roadStreet Publishing Group, LLC.
avage, Minnesota, USA
Broadstreetpublishing.com

THE POWER OF PRAYER *(A Christian Classic Devotional)*

9781424571314
9781424571321 eBook

Devotional entries compiled by Sara Perry.

Typesetting and design by Garborg Design Works | garborgdesign.com
Editorial services by Michelle Winger | literallyprecise.com

Printed in China.

25 26 27 28 29 30 31 7 6 5 4 3 2 1

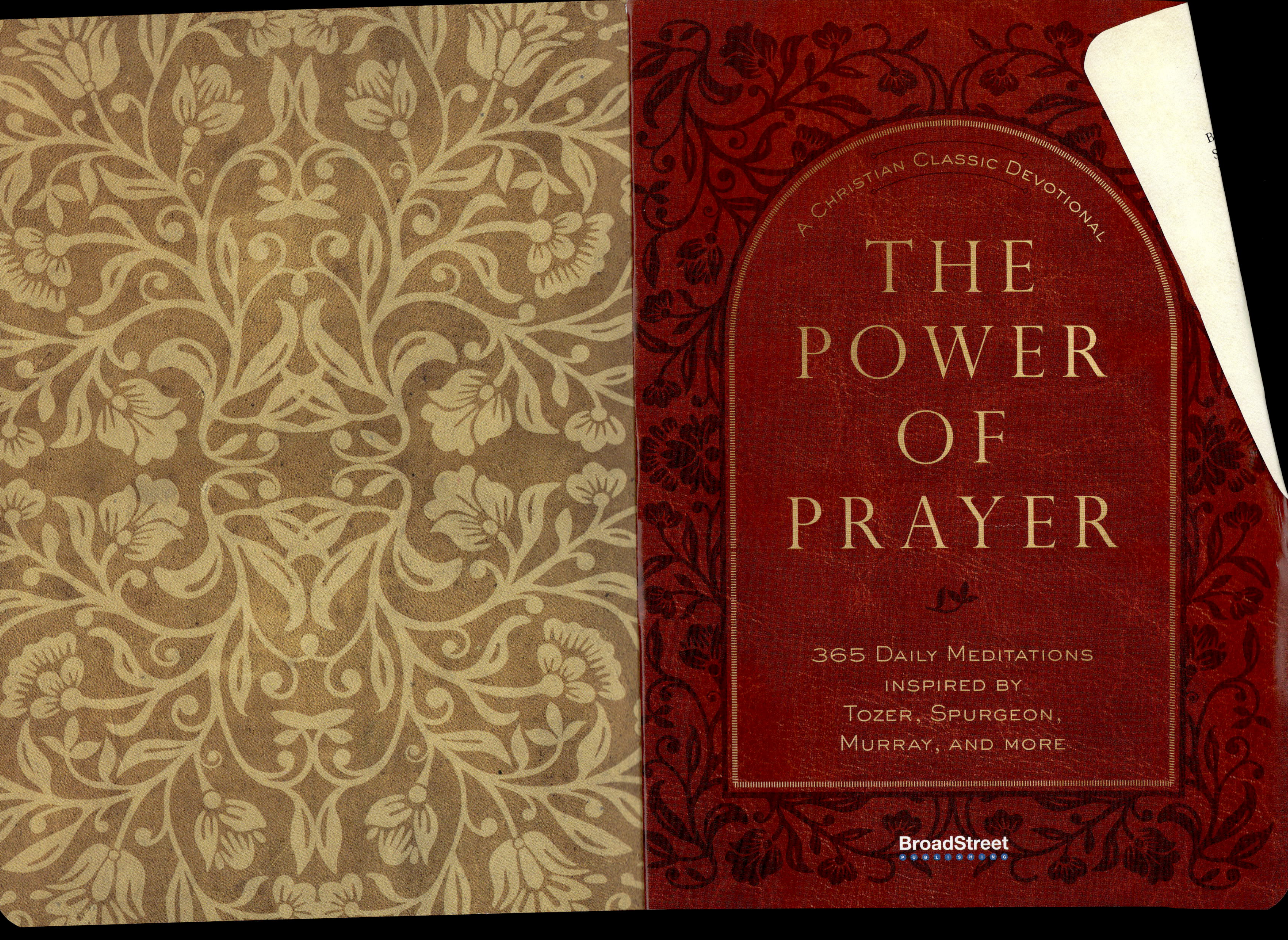

A Christian Classic Devotional
THE POWER OF PRAYER
365 Daily Meditations inspired by Tozer, Spurgeon, Murray, and more
BroadStreet
PUBLISHING

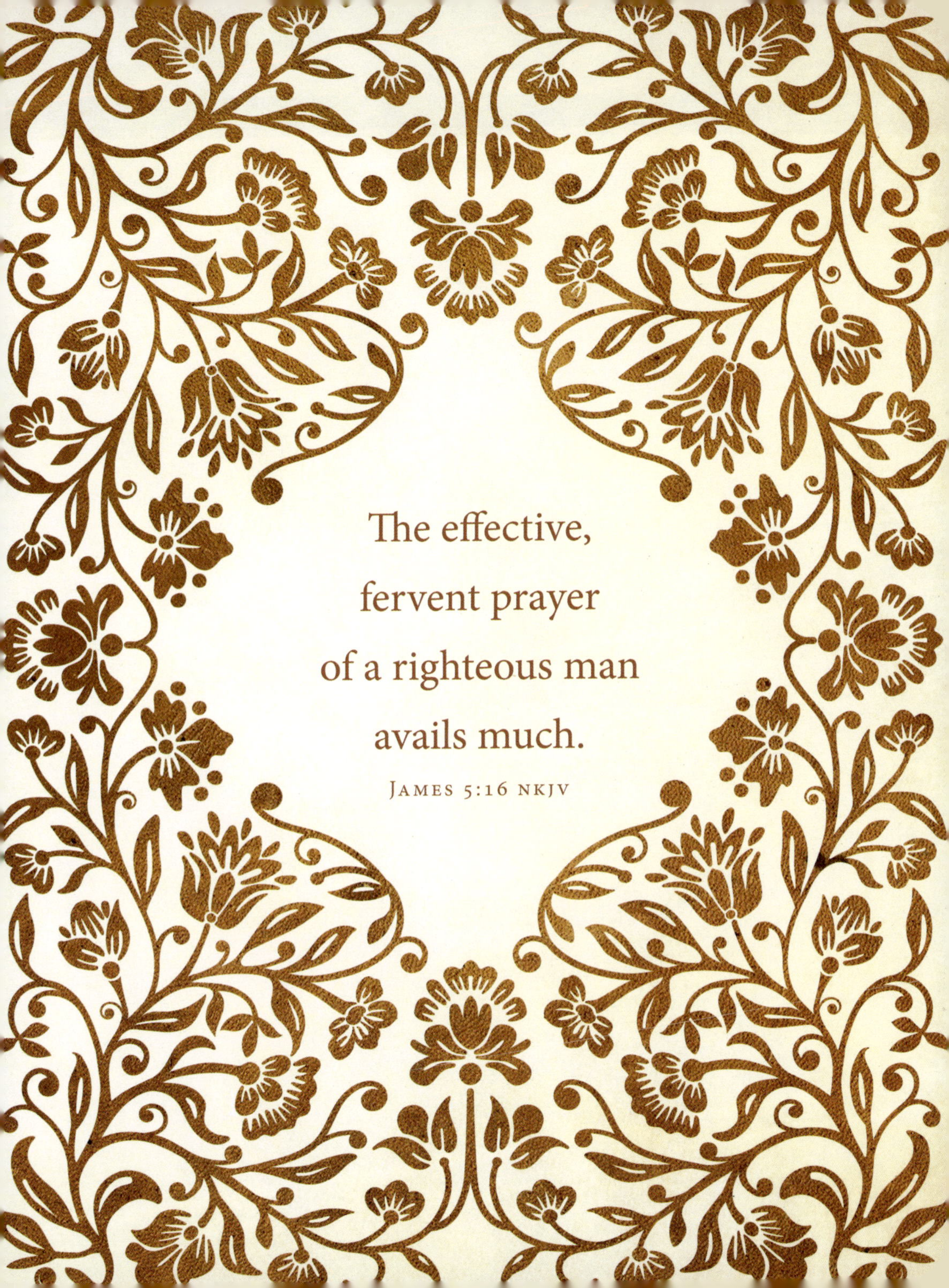
The effective,
fervent prayer
of a righteous man
avails much.
James 5:16 NKJV

INTRODUCTION

Unlock the transformative power of prayer with this classic daily devotional.

The Power of Prayer is a beautifully crafted collection of meditations that invites you into a deeper, more intimate walk with God. It offers wisdom and insights drawn from some of Christianity's most profound voices, including Spurgeon, Murray, Augustine, Bounds, Tozer, and other timeless spiritual leaders.

Each day's reading will inspire, challenge, and guide you to cultivate a richer prayer life, grounding you in the truth that prayer is not just a practice but the pathway to communion with your Creator. Whether you are new to prayer or a prayer closet veteran, these meditations will provide daily nourishment for your spirit.

Discover the power of persistent prayer and gain practical guidance and encouragement from Christian classics that have withstood the test of time. Let this devotional be your companion on the journey to greater intimacy with God, as you tap into the deep well of prayer's power and experience the life-changing presence of the Holy Spirit.

TEACH US TO PRAY

"When you pray, say:
Our Father in heaven,
Hallowed be Your name.
Your kingdom come.
Your will be done
On earth as it is in heaven."

LUKE 11:2 NKJV

This wonderful prayer was dictated by our Lord in reply to the question on the part of His disciples, "Lord, teach us to pray." His answer was to bid them pray. This is the only way we shall ever learn to pray, by just beginning to do it. —A.B. Simpson, The Life of Prayer

Prayer is not a hard language to learn, nor is it something you have to master before you do it. Prayer is communication with your heavenly Father. The only way to learn how to pray is by praying. You don't have to read up on it, and you don't have to waver in it either. The more you practice it, the more natural it will become.

The most solid foundation of prayer is the one that Jesus himself taught his disciples. If you don't know what to say, repeat Jesus' words found in Luke 11:2-4. Your Father listens to your prayer, and he will answer you.

Today, pray the Lord's Prayer.

KEEP PRAYING

Pray in the Spirit on all occasions with all kinds of prayers and requests. With this in mind, be alert and always keep on praying for all the Lord's people.
EPHESIANS 6:18 NIV

I must pray, pray, pray. I must put all my energy and all my heart into prayer. Whatever else I do, I must pray. —R. A. Torrey, How to Pray

Prayer is not something saved for special occasions or our worst days. When we are sick, yes, we should pray. When the world is haywire, let's pray. But we must not forget to pray when times are good, and we are filled with love. Let us pray for those around us, as well as for the goodness of God to meet us in every season.

Prayer is a practice that is meant for every day. It is as vital to our soul's health as food, water, and sun is to our body's well-being. We need connection with God to thrive. Our prayers will change in tenor and tone, but the connection to God remains the same. He is faithful, unchanging, and always available to his children!

Pray to God whenever you think of it today.

GREATER THINGS

"As heaven is higher than earth,
so my ways are higher than your ways,
and my thoughts than your thoughts."
ISAIAH 55:9 CSB

Do not bring before God stinted petitions and narrow desires, and say, "Lord, do according to these," but, remember, as high as the heavens are above the earth, so high are his ways above your ways, and his thoughts above your thoughts, and ask, therefore, after a God-like sort, ask for great things, for you are before the throne of grace, for then he would do for us exceeding abundantly above what we ask or even think. —C. H. Spurgeon, The Throne of Grace

When you come before the throne of grace, you approach the King who is above every ruler and power of this world. He is able to do far more than you can imagine, and he delights in answering the prayers of his children. Why not take your prayers to God and hold them up to him in hope?

You don't have to keep your prayers small. No! Ask for the greater things: mountains moved, bodies healed, and hopes fulfilled. Nothing is impossible for him.

How freely do you ask God for greater things—the things of his kingdom?

CHILDREN OF GOD

The Spirit we received does not make us slaves again to fear; it makes us children of God. With that Spirit we cry out, "Father."

ROMANS 8:15 NCV

All true prayer begins in the recognition of the Father. It is not the cry of nature to an unknown God, but the intelligent converse of a child with his heavenly Father. —A.B. Simpson, The Life of Prayer

God is not a far-off figure who is out of touch with the world or what is going on in it. He is not a dictator, bossing us around and expecting us to fall in line without question. He is not simply a figurehead without power to enact change. He is a Father, and we are his beloved children.

When we come to God through prayer, we can pour out our hearts to him without fear. He wants us to share our lives, our troubles, and our joys with him. We don't have to edit ourselves. He knows our hearts already, and to speak the truth of what is in us to the God who not only knows but loves us is powerful.

Talk to God like the loving, interested, invested Father he is.

POWERFUL PRAYER

The Lord is far from the wicked,
but he hears the prayer of the righteous.
Proverbs 15:29 ESV

No amount of money, genius, or culture can move things for God. Holiness energizing the soul, the whole man aflame with love, with desire for more faith, more prayer, more zeal, more consecration—this is the secret of power. —E. M. Bounds, Power Through Prayer

We cannot convince God to listen to us with what we offer him. Power, money, and influence do not move his heart. What moves God's heart is love, humility, the desire to know him, and a hunger for wisdom.

You don't have to dress yourself up for God to earn his attention. You don't have to prove yourself to him either. He delights in coming close to the seeking heart. He shows himself to those who wait on him. Don't follow the ways of this world and think you've found the answer to power. God's power is better than any you could find in halls of influence, without corruption, manipulation, or greed.

Humble yourself before God and let love lead your prayer.

ASK MUCH

"Ask, and it will be given to you; seek, and you will find; knock, and it will be opened to you. For everyone who asks receives, and the one who seeks finds, and to the one who knocks it will be opened."
MATTHEW 7:7-8 NASB

Fellow-laborers in His vineyard, it is quite evident that our Master desires us to ask, and to ask much. He tells us we glorify God by doing so!
—Anonymous, Kneeling Christian

We don't have to wait around helplessly wondering whether God will show up and meet us or not. Ask, and it will be given. Seek, and you will find. Knock, and the door will be opened. Waiting seasons don't necessitate seasons of silence. No, let's bring our questions, our longings, and our requests before our heavenly Master, our good and gracious Savior!

When we have questions, we don't have to hide them from God. When we have needs, we don't have to ignore them. Faith brings our lack and holds it up to God's faithfulness. Let's not forget to ask, and ask much. God honors the seeking heart, always, and he will meet us in our need.

Do you hesitate to ask God for what you need in prayer?

FORGIVENESS FIRST

"When you are praying, first forgive anyone you are holding a grudge against, so that your Father in heaven will forgive your sins, too."
MARK 11:25 NLT

Every prayer rests upon our faith in God's pardoning grace. If God dealt with us after our sins, not one prayer could be heard. Pardon opens the door to all God's love and blessing: because God has pardoned all our sin, our prayer can prevail to obtain all we need. The deep sure ground of answer to prayer is God's forgiving love.
—Andrew Murray, With Christ in the School of Prayer

God's grace gives us freedom. He forgives us our sins, and we come before him without the weight of guilt, fear, or shame. We are to follow his example in our own hearts and lives. When we choose to forgive others as he has forgiven us, we live from the freedom of his gracious love.

Let's not overlook the importance of forgiving those we hold grudges against. If there is a bitter root in our hearts, it will keep us from the freedom Christ offers. As we offer Jesus our open hearts and choose to forgive the failings of others, we make room to receive what we truly desire from God.

Consider the grudges you may be holding on to (even toward yourself). Will you forgive today?

I AM

Be exalted, O God, above the heavens;
Let Your glory be above all the earth.
PSALM 57:5 NKJV

When God would make His Name known to mankind He could find no better word than "I AM." When He speaks in the first person He says, "I AM"; when we speak of Him we say, "He is"; when we speak to Him we say, "Thou art." Everyone and everything else measures from that fixed point. "I am that I am," says God, "I change not."
—A.W. Tozer, The Pursuit of God

God is worthy of our praise, no matter the season or circumstances of our lives. He is all that we could ever dream, and he is so much more. God, the exalted one, is glorious and good. We cannot exaggerate his goodness, nor can we praise him enough.

When we pray, let's not overlook his majesty or power. He is faithful, unchanging, and true. He is that he is, and he will always be. He is present, he is perfect, and he is waiting for us to turn our attention to him even now. Let's give him our adoration and praise.

Let praise be your prayer right now.

MOVING GOD'S HEART

Do not be anxious about anything, but in every situation, by prayer and petition, with thanksgiving, present your requests to God.
PHILIPPIANS 4:6 NIV

Prayer affects men by affecting God. Prayer moves men because it moves God to move men. Prayer influences men by influencing God to influence them. Prayer moves the hand that moves the world.
—E. M. Bounds, The Possibilities of Prayer

Isn't it comforting to know that your prayers move the heart of God? Not only that, but he uses your prayers to influence others. There is every reason to pray, no matter the situation, your feelings about it, or your energy. You always have access to God through prayer. How often do you connect to him through it?

You can give God your anxieties and leave them there. He knows exactly what to do in each and every situation. He has solutions for your problems, strength for your weakness, and overwhelming love to fill every need. Present your requests to God, and let him move. Let him do what he does best. You don't have to control a thing.

Let every anxious thought become a prayer and a petition.

TURN TOWARD HIM

Rejoice always, pray constantly, give thanks in everything; for this is God's will for you in Christ Jesus.

1 THESSALONIANS 5:16-18 CSB

You need not utterly despair even of those who for the present "turn again and rend you." For if all your arguments and persuasives fail, there is yet another remedy left, and one that is frequently found effectual, when no other method avails. This is prayer.
—John Wesley, Upon Our Lord's Sermon on the Mount

The consistent turning of our hearts to the Lord is what prayer is. No matter where we are in the world, no matter what is going on in or around us, God is available. He is ready to receive us as we come to him, and he is present in our midst by his Holy Spirit.

God's will isn't that we struggle on our own. It's not that we would pick ourselves up by the bootstraps. It's not for us to keep striving until we break. The invitation—his hope—is that we'll lean on him. None of us can earn our salvation, and we don't have to try to keep ourselves in his good graces. We are his children, and he is our loving Father. In all things, let's rejoice, pray, and give thanks.

Are you trying to prove yourself to God, or have you pressed in to know him as a good Father?

GRACE ENTHRONED

Let us then with confidence draw near to the throne of grace, that we may receive mercy and find grace to help in time of need.
HEBREWS 4:16 ESV

The throne of grace. The word grows as I turn it over in my mind, and to me it is a most delightful reflection that if I come to the throne of God in prayer, I may feel a thousand defects, but yet there is hope.
—C. H. Spurgeon, The Throne of Grace

We don't have to dress ourselves up before God or tidy up our emotions before approaching him in prayer. He already sees and knows us as we are. Why should we pretend? No, he welcomes us with grace and mercy, and he is ready to restore our hope, our strength, and our peace in his presence.

Whenever we are in need, that's a good time to go to God. Grace isn't a limited resource. God's generosity is greater than we can imagine. We cannot deplete his stores of mercy or exhaust his gracious patience. He is always ready to help us in our time of need (even if that is every day!).

Do you limit your prayers, thinking you're being a bother? Go with confidence to the throne of grace as many times as you need.

HOLY SPIRIT HELP

Then we can continue to pray and to teach the word of God.
ACTS 6:4 NCV

Every provision is made for us. But only the Holy Spirit can stir us up to take hold of God. And if we will but yield ourselves to the Spirit's promptings we shall most assuredly follow the example of the apostles of old, who gave themselves to prayer, and continued steadfastly in prayer. —Anonymous, Kneeling Christian

Prayer is a practice, and it becomes more natural by repetition. The more we turn our hearts to the Lord, the more the Spirit stirs and directs our attention to God's desires. If we want to have solid prayer lives, we cannot wait around for it to one day click. With a little intention and action, we can yield our hearts to God, and he will stir up a hunger to continue.

Knowing that the Holy Spirit is our help, we don't have to wait a moment longer to put prayer into practice. Even when we don't know what to pray for, the Holy Spirit intercedes on our behalf. When we surrender ourselves to the Spirit's promptings, we will know the power of God in our hearts, minds, and lives.

Ask the Holy Spirit to move in your heart as you pray.

REST IN GOD

Truly my soul finds rest in God;
my salvation comes from him.
Truly he is my rock and my salvation;
he is my fortress, I will never be shaken.
PSALM 62:1-2 NIV

You have made us for yourself, O Lord, and our hearts are restless until they rest in you. —St. Augustine, Confessions

It is possible to find rest in God each and every day. We don't have to bear our burdens, no matter how weighty they are, alone. Christ is our rock and our salvation, and when we make our home in his love, he wraps around us with the peace of his presence.

Jesus said in Matthew 11:28, "Come to me, all you who are weary and burdened, and I will give you rest." When your heart is weighed down by the burdens of this life, come to Jesus. Bring him everything you carry, and lay them at his feet. He will care for you, offer you the strength of his grace, and revive you in his love. You were made out of love, and to love you return. Find your rest in your Creator.

Bring every worry, fear, and burden to the Lord today.

WORDLESS PRAYERS

The sacrifices of God are a broken spirit;
A broken and a contrite heart, God, You will not despise.
PSALM 51:17 NASB

In prayer, it is better to have a heart without words than words without a heart. —John Bunyan, The Pilgrim's Progress

When you don't have words to pray, don't be discouraged. God reads the prayers of your heart as you turn your attention toward him. Romans 8:26 promises, "the Spirit also helps our weakness; for we do not know what to pray for as we should, but the Spirit Himself intercedes for us with groanings too deep for words."

When our words fail, the Holy Spirit steps in and prays on our behalf. What a beautiful God, that we can trust him to partner with us in prayer, not only in what we ask, but also in the things we don't have language to petition him for.

When you don't have the words to convey your prayers, invite the Holy Spirit to pray on your behalf.

WHOLEHEARTED TRUST

Trust in the LORD with all your heart;
do not depend on your own understanding.
PROVERBS 3:5 NLT

It is not for us to know what the future holds, but to trust in God's purpose for us, and prayer is a way to live into that trust.
—Dietrich Bonhoeffer, Letters and Papers from Prison

Prayer isn't just about communicating with God. It's not only about asking him for what we need, nor is it about appeasing him. He is already full of love, and he wants us to know the extent of his faithfulness. Prayer helps us build our relationship with him, and it is a practice of trust.

When do you most pray to God? Is it when you are feeling settled and happy, or is it in the more tumultuous or unknown times of life? Ideally, we pray in every season. However, when we feel the pressures of life, we may feel the need to reach out to the Lord more. God is faithful at all times, and he never changes. Prayer moves us closer to his presence, and it offers peace through placing our trust in God's unfailing nature.

When you pray today, actively put your trust in God's purposes for you, and ultimately, in his faithfulness to his nature.

WHAT YOU NEED

"Your Father knows the things you have need of before you ask Him."
MATTHEW 6:8 NKJV

We must not think that [God] takes no notice of us, when He does not answer our wishes: for He has a right to distinguish what we actually need. —John Calvin, Commentary on the Gospel of Matthew

You don't have to beg God to provide for your needs. He already knows all that you require, and he won't hesitate to care for you. Jesus' reassuring words to his followers are the same he speaks to us today.

So, what does that mean when what we want goes unmet? Let's take a step back from our expectations and ask God to shine the light of his wisdom on our minds and hearts. Though we might think we know how God should answer our prayers, God's solutions are thorough. He considers details that we are not aware of. Let's trust him even when we don't understand.

Have you ever looked back through the lens of hindsight and been thankful God didn't answer your prayer the way you thought he should?

DRAWN TO JESUS

"No one can come to me unless the Father who sent me draws them, and I will raise them up at the last day."

JOHN 6:44 NIV

We pursue God because, and only because, He has first put an urge within us that spurs us to the pursuit. "No man can come to me," said our Lord, "except the Father which hath sent me draw him," and it is by this very prevenient drawing that God takes from us every vestige of credit for the act of coming. —A.W. Tozer, The Pursuit of God

If you have ever questioned the authenticity of your desire for God, may today's verse and quote put your mind at rest. God drew you to himself before you knew him. He called you before you knew his voice. Whatever desire you feel, it originated in the heart of God. And he loves you! He welcomes you with open arms no matter when or how you come to him.

Let your pursuit of the Lord be uninhibited. Don't hesitate in his presence, for he draws you to himself with loving-kindness. Your pursuit of God is not something to use as a measuring stick against others. Don't compare your journey with anyone else's. Just look to the one who draws you with mercy.

Let your heart be led in love as you pray, and let your doubts fall away in his presence.

DIRECT YOUR GAZE

Looking to Jesus, the founder and perfecter of our faith, who for the joy that was set before him endured the cross, despising the shame, and is seated at the right hand of the throne of God.
HEBREWS 12:2 ESV

Faith is not a once-done act, but a continuous gaze of the heart at the Triune God. Believing, then, is directing the heart's attention to Jesus. It is lifting the mind to "behold the Lamb of God," and never ceasing that beholding for the rest of our lives. —A.W. Tozer, The Pursuit of God

Prayer is an act of faith, directing the heart's attention to Jesus. We behold the Son of God with the eyes of our hearts, and we are transformed by his character. The more we offer God our attention, the more our hearts are filled with the glory of his presence.

Even when we experience the hardest days, God's presence is as near to us as the skin on our bones. His peace is as life giving as the air in our lungs. With thoughtful intention, let's make prayer a practice, and turn our attention to the one who watches over us continually. He will never leave us, and he is always available to hear our prayers.

Continually turn the gaze of your heart toward the Lord today. Whenever you think of it, pray!

MAKE PRAYER A PRIORITY

Very early in the morning, while it was still dark, he got up, went out, and made his way to a deserted place; and there he was praying.
MARK 1:35 CSB

There is a still weightier reason for this constant, persistent, sleepless, overcoming prayer. It is, prayer occupied a very prominent place and played a very important part in the earthly life of our Lord.
—R. A. Torrey, How to Pray

Jesus was sure to keep prayer an important part of his routine. Why do you think this is? Do you suppose it was an obligation he felt? Or rather an opportunity to connect with his heavenly Father? In the secret place of prayer, Jesus could pour his heart out to God. It's the same for us.

When you awake and are alone in the quiet, what if you got up and used that time for prayer? You may not be able to rearrange much in your already busy schedule, but you can follow the example of Jesus and carve out time to connect with your Father. Whether in the morning or the evening, or anytime that is possible, get up, get alone, and pour your heart out to God.

Spend time in the secret place of prayer with your God.

COMMUNAL PRAYER

"Also, I tell you that if two of you on earth agree about something and pray for it, it will be done for you by my Father in heaven. This is true because if two or three people come together in my name, I am there with them."

Matthew 18:19-20 NCV

You have need not only of secret solitary, but also of public united prayer. And He gives us a very special promise for the united prayer of two or three who agree in what they ask. As a tree has its root hidden in the ground and its stem growing up into the sunlight, so prayer needs equally for its full development the hidden secrecy in which the soul meets God alone, and the public fellowship with those who find in the name of Jesus their common meeting-place.
—Andrew Murray, With Christ in the School of Prayer

We need both solitary prayer and communal times of prayer. In the former, you can empty your heart before God. In the latter, you come together in agreement for God to move in specific ways. The united prayers of God's people are powerful!

You don't need a large group to pray communally. You can do it with even one other person. Partnered prayer can be a mighty comfort, grace, and strength in the moment.

Seek out or offer prayer to another today.

UNFAILING MERCY

The Lord's acts of mercy indeed do not end,
For His compassions do not fail.
Lamentations 3:22 NASB

Seek a suitable time for thy meditation, and think frequently of the mercies of God to thee. —Thomas à Kempis, The Imitation of Christ

The more we focus on God's goodness, the more readily we recognize it in our lives. This isn't just something we say, it is how our minds work. This is why it's so important to direct our thoughts to the Lord and to remember his mercies toward us.

Meditative prayer is not a new way to pray. Also known as contemplative prayer, it focuses on stillness and inner reflection. Joshua 1:8 says, "You shall meditate on [the Book of the Law] day and night." When we direct our thoughts and move our attention toward God and his Word, our understanding of who he is will deepen. The more we reflect on his faithfulness, his mercy, and his provision in our lives, the more grateful we will become in response.

Spend time in meditation, remembering the specific kindnesses of God toward you.

UNCHANGING ONE

God is not a man, so he does not lie.
He is not human, so he does not change his mind.
NUMBERS 23:19 NLT

We ought, once for all, heartily to put our whole trust in God, and make a total surrender of ourselves to Him, secure that He would not deceive us. —Brother Lawrence, The Practice of the Presence of God

Prayer is an act of putting our trust in the unchanging God. He is faithful to do all that he has promised, and he does not change his mind. What he says, he follows through with. What he promises, he does. It may not be in our timing, but as the Scripture says, "A day is like a thousand years to the Lord, and a thousand years is like a day" (2 Peter 3:8).

God's faithfulness is his character, and he will not change like the shifting winds of this world or of popular opinion. He cannot be talked out of his love, and he will not be convinced of a lie. He is the way, the truth, and the life, and you can trust that his heart and eyes are unclouded from manipulation. If you are waiting on God to move, don't lose heart. He will do what he promised to do.

Surrender yourself to God in prayer as you actively choose to trust his timing.

LAW OF LOVE

"In everything, do to others what you would have them do to you, for this sums up the Law and the Prophets."
MATTHEW 7:12 NKJV

The need of help outside of man being so great, man's natural inability to always judge kindly, justly, and truly, and to act the Golden Rule, so prayer is enjoined by Christ to enable man to act in all these things according to the Divine will. By prayer, the ability is secured to feel the law of love, to speak according to the law of love, and to do everything in harmony with the law of love.
—E. M. Bounds, The Possibilities of Prayer

The law of love is clearly spelled out in what we call The Golden Rule. It encompasses the whole of the Old Testament Law and Prophets. When we choose to walk in the ways of Christ, we cannot ignore the example of his incomparable kindness, overwhelming mercy, and gracious generosity.

When we begin to use our faith as an excuse for our lack of love, we miss the point entirely. Love turns the other cheek. It helps those who others overlook. It invites in and cares for the poor, those without family, and the refugee. If this is hard, we must pray. Pray for more of God's love to move in our hearts.

Pray for your actions to line up with the law of Christ's love.

EVER PRESENT

Where can I go from your Spirit?
Where can I flee from your presence?
Psalm 139:7 NIV

Wherever we are, God is here. There is no place, there can be no place, where He is not… No point is nearer to God than any other point. It is exactly as near to God from any place as it is from any other place. No one is in mere distance any further from or any nearer to God than any other person is. —A.W. Tozer, The Pursuit of God

What a relief it is to know that we don't have to worry about straying from God's presence. Wherever we are, there he is. We can't outrun his love, and we can't lose his Spirit. Just as the air always surrounds us, so God's presence is near from birth to death.

As you pray, remember how close God is. Turn your attention to the way the air fills your lungs as you breathe it in. Let it serve as a reminder that God's presence is as close. Combine your deep breathing with prayers of meditation on his Word. It will help calm your anxiety and focus your attention on God.

Inhale: Lord, my heart searches for you. Exhale: You are with me.

PROMISED PEACE

The peace of God, which surpasses all understanding, will guard your hearts and your minds in Christ Jesus.
Philippians 4:7 esv

Just keep in constant touch with God, and when any trouble or vexation, great or small, comes up, speak to Him about it, never forgetting to return thanks for what He has already done.
—R. A. Torrey, How to Pray

Why do we pray? Is it to put on a show for God or others? Is it so we feel more spiritual? Prayer is not a one-sided act. We are the prayers, God is the hearer. It is an act of relational connection, and there is a divine exchange that occurs through it. It doesn't end when we say "Amen."

We use prayer as a conversation, thanking God for what he does as we trust him with what we present to him. And his Spirit moves in response, giving us peace that guards our hearts and minds. His presence speaks peace, wisdom, and power to our bodies, and we receive what he so willingly offers.

When you pray today, end with thanks and take time to receive what the Holy Spirit offers.

FAITHFUL FRIEND

"I no longer call you servants, because a servant does not know what his master is doing. But I call you friends, because I have made known to you everything I heard from my Father."
John 15:15 NCV

He is a Friend, not only in season, but at all seasons, and at the most unseasonable times. The peculiarity of God's grace is that He helps when man would refuse to help, and its highest trophies are associated with hours when mercy seemed long past and hope forever dead.
—A.B. Simpson, The Life of Prayer

There is never a bad time to show up at God's door. You can come to him in the middle of the night, looking a mess, and he will open the door to his presence. As soon as you turn to him, in fact, you will discover that he is already nearer than you knew.

Jesus is the best of friends. He doesn't leave when you are in a hard spot. He is ever faithful, ever present, and ever loving. Why would you stay away from him when he has everything you need? He's got the wisdom, grace, patience, clarity, and peace you're looking for.

Spend time in prayer with your faithful Friend.

ELEVATED ACTS

Brothers and sisters, pray for us that the word of the Lord may spread rapidly and be honored, just as it was with you.
2 THESSALONIANS 3:1 CSB

Prayer is no trifle. It is an eminent and elevated act. It is a high and wondrous privilege. —C. H. Spurgeon, The Throne of Grace

Prayer is a holy act, and yet it is one of the simplest ways we put our faith into practice. It is a wonderful privilege to be able to come before the Lord with boldness. We offer him our heartfelt trust as we petition him for the needs of others.

How often do you pray for others? When you join your prayer to God's generous heart, he responds in faithfulness. It is no small thing to pray for God's intervention and wisdom when we don't know what to do. It is a high and wondrous privilege, an eminent and elevated act. It joins our hearts to God's purposes. Why would we brush it aside, when faith-filled prayer has the ability to move mountains?

Spend time praying for others today.

SEEK AND FIND

"Blessed are those who hunger and thirst for righteousness, for they will be satisfied."
MATTHEW 5:6 NASB

The heart which is behindhand in seeking God in the morning has lost its relish for God. David's heart was ardent after God. He hungered and thirsted after God, and so he sought God early, before daylight.
—E. M. Bounds, Power Through Prayer

A prayerful heart reaches for the Lord in constant connection. We don't have to only pray during a dedicated time in our day. We can pray throughout, sending God our heart's cries, whispers, and attention. As we turn our attention to him, even in stolen moments, he meets us.

Still, there is something to be said about starting our days by searching for the Lord. No matter the time we wake up, as our consciousness awakens, let us position our gaze toward God. A simple, "Thank you, Lord, for this new day" is enough to start us off right. When we ask him to reveal his goodness, his presence, and his faithfulness, we open the eyes of our hearts to look for his marks of mercy. Those who hunger and thirst will be satisfied.

Each morning, before you even open your eyes, start your day with prayer.

PASSIONATE PURSUIT

O God, you are my God;
I earnestly search for you.
My soul thirsts for you;
my whole body longs for you.
PSALM 63:1 NLT

To have found God and still to pursue Him is the soul's paradox of love.
—A.W. Tozer, The Pursuit of God

The more we get to know the goodness of God's character, the more we love him. His kindness is irresistible! David's passionate pursuit of God was not based in fear or mistrust. It was rooted in love.

God's love satisfies our souls and feeds our hunger for him at the same time. Consider what it's like to be in love. You spend as much time as you can with the person, and when you're apart, you want to be around them still! We can know this kind of love with the Lord with a notable exception: he will never leave us, disappoint us, or mislead us. His love is perfect, and he is so worthy of our continual pursuit.

Ask the Lord to fill your heart with his love as you look to him.

BETTER STILL

The word of God is living and powerful, and sharper than any two-edged sword, piercing even to the division of soul and spirit, and of joints and marrow, and is a discerner of the thoughts and intents of the heart.

HEBREWS 4:12 NKJV

What God says is best, is best, though all the men in the world are against it. —John Bunyan, The Pilgrim's Progress

God's Word is sharp. It is always right, and it's right on time. God's wisdom doesn't expire with the ages. His truth is based in his faithful character, and that means it is timeless. What good news this is for us!

The law of God's love is the same powerful measure we use today. Christ displayed the goodness of his Father in his ministry. He lived out the mercy of God and displayed his power through incredible miracles. As we pray, let's not be unaware of the foundation of God's truth: his limitless love. As we align our lives with Jesus' ways, we move toward the best God has for us. It's even better than what we could ask for.

Ask the Lord to help you walk in his ways even when it costs you something.

BEHOLD HIM

I have seen you in the sanctuary
and beheld your power and your glory.
Psalm 63:2 niv

God comes down to us by his Spirit, and we go up to him by prayer.
—Thomas Watson, The Ten Commandments

Prayer is an active exchange with the Holy Spirit. His presence draws us close to the heart of the Father, and it is as if there is no distance between us as we pour out our hearts to the Creator of our souls.

You can think of prayer as an act of beholding God. When you turn your attention to his nature, and listen for his voice, you will encounter his presence. The old hymn comes to mind, "Turn your eyes upon Jesus, look full in his wonderful face, and the things of earth will grow strangely dim, in the light of his glory and grace." Turn your eyes toward your Savior today, and behold the beauty of his loving countenance!

Prayerfully worship your Savior today.

KNOWING GOD

"Let him who boasts boast in this, that he understands and knows me, that I am the LORD who practices steadfast love, justice, and righteousness in the earth. For in these things I delight," declares the LORD.

JEREMIAH 9:24 ESV

Those who know God the best are the richest and most powerful in prayer. Little acquaintance with God, and strangeness and coldness to Him, make prayer a rare and feeble thing.
—E. M. Bounds, Power Through Prayer

Knowing God is one of the greatest benefits of a robust prayer life. Similarly, the more we know God through his Word and fellowship with his Spirit, the more our prayer lives are enriched. Our prayers become surer as we get to know what he is like.

Today's verse is clear. When we align our prayers with God's character, we don't have to question whether he will answer them. He is faithful and just, and he will act according to the power of his faithful love. Go ahead, get to know him more, and your prayer life will benefit!

Pray for a deeper relationship with the Lord and a deeper understanding of his character.

DAILY SUSTENANCE

"Give us this day our daily bread."
Matthew 6:11 NASB

"Give us this day our daily bread," gives to every child of God the right to claim a Father's supporting and providing love. It is wonderful how much spiritual blessing we get by praying and trusting for temporal needs. —A.B. Simpson, The Life of Prayer

We don't always feel the urgent need for God's provision, but when we do, we don't have to worry. We can settle our hearts as we pray like Jesus taught his disciples to pray. "Give us this day our daily bread," is a simple, faith-filled request that our heavenly Father honors. God is good, and he is faithful. We don't have to beg him for what we need; he provides for his children.

When you feel the tendrils of worry about the future squeezing your heart, refocus on today. What do you need for this moment? What do you need to get through this very day? Thank God for today's provision, and trust him with tomorrow's. He will take care of you.

Ask the Lord for provision, and for the eyes to see how he takes care of you.

FAITH TO ASK

"LORD, answer my prayer so these people will know that you, LORD, are God and that you will change their minds." Then fire from the LORD came down and burned the sacrifice, the wood, the stones, and the ground around the altar. It also dried up the water in the ditch.

1 KINGS 18:37-38 NCV

Elijah had the promise that God would send the rain, but no promise that He would send the fire. But by faith and prayer he obtained the fire, as well as the rain, but the fire came first.
—E. M. Bounds, The Possibilities of Prayer

Elijah didn't keep his prayers to the promise he already had. He moved in boldness, and he asked the Lord to reveal his power to the people. When we have a promise from the Lord, we can surely stand upon it.

God's power is limitless, and so is his love. We don't have to be timid about entering his courts or pursuing his presence. The Lord is patient with us, for he knows us. The surer we become of his goodness, the more our prayers will reflect his kindness, and our faith will match his faithfulness.

How do you long to see God move? Pray and ask him to do it.

GOD'S WORK

It is God who is working in you both to will and to work according to his good purpose.
PHILIPPIANS 2:13 CSB

I used to ask God to help me. Then I asked if I might help Him. I ended up by asking Him to do His work through me.
—James Hudson Taylor, Hudson Taylor's Spiritual Secret

Prayer is partnership with the King. He is above the rulers of this world, and his ways are better than the best of men. He is slow to anger, patient in love, and generous in grace. He leads in mercy always, and he will not leave you to fight your own battles.

Every impulse toward doing good, being generous, courageously standing for justice, and reaching out to a neighbor in need reflects God's love at work in your heart. Yes, God will provide for you as his child, but that's not where your prayer life or partnership ends. He empowers you by his grace to live out his mercy in practical ways.

Ask the Lord what you can do today to partner with him.

ALERT AND THANKFUL

Devote yourselves to prayer with an alert mind and a thankful heart.
COLOSSIANS 4:2

To be a Christian without prayer is no more possible than to be alive without breathing. —Martin Luther, Large Catechism

Prayer is the open door to God's throne. It is the thread of communication that binds us to his heart. Perhaps you have known the tension that builds from mulling over a conversation you need to have. There is no relief until the words that need to be said are out. Then, and only then, does the unknown become known in how the person receives you.

Many of us have one-sided conversations in our minds about God, but we do not take them to him in prayer. What relief we find as we pour out what we've been holding back, and let him speak to the questions and vulnerability we have laid before him. There is comfort, wisdom, and clarity in the truth of his Word and consistent nature. Let's not be closed off in prayer. When we remain alert, open, and thankful, our prayer lives become as natural as breathing.

Bring God the things you've been holding off asking him.

SOURCE OF STRENGTH

Those who wait on the LORD
Shall renew their strength;
They shall mount up with wings like eagles,
They shall run and not be weary,
They shall walk and not faint.
ISAIAH 40:31 NKJV

Wise is he in the day of trouble who knows his true source of strength and who fails not to pray. —E. M. Bounds, The Essentials of Prayer

God is present in our troubles, and he always leads us by the power of his grace. We are not alone—ever! Prayer connects our needy hearts to God's ready provision. He offers us strength to stand, and he gives courage to those who wait.

If you find yourself waiting on God's help, pray. When you don't know what to do, turn to the Lord. When you are weak, afraid, or unsure, turn your attention to your Maker. He will not let you down. Your strength will be renewed as you wait, giving you endurance to keep going and hope that will sustain you.

When you find yourself waiting, pray. Ask for God's gracious strength.

SOWING SEEDS

"The seed falling on good soil refers to someone who hears the word and understands it. This is the one who produces a crop, yielding a hundred, sixty or thirty times what was sown."
MATTHEW 13:23 NIV

A beginner must look on himself as one setting out to make a garden for his Lord's pleasure, on most unfruitful soil which abounds in weeds. His majesty roots up the weeds and will put in good plants instead. Let us reckon that this is already done when the soul decides to practice prayer and has begun to do so.
—St. Teresa of Ávila, The Life of Teresa of Jesus

Every prayer acts as a tilling of the soil of your heart. When you practice prayer, turning your attention to the Lord and offering him your cares, he sows seeds of grace. The fruit of the Spirit doesn't appear out of nowhere. It begins as a seed, and as you water it and give it the light it needs, it grows and matures.

If you want to grow in wisdom and in the ways of the Lord, prayer is a necessary practice. It isn't difficult, and it doesn't require more than what you have to offer right in this very moment. Partner with the Spirit's work and turn over the soil of your heart as you pray.

Make prayer a practice just as you would water the plants in your garden.

AS NATURAL AS BREATHING

Rejoice in hope, be patient in tribulation, be constant in prayer.
Romans 12:12 ESV

Prayer is not a hard requirement—it is the natural duty of a creature to its creator, the simplest homage that human need can pay to divine liberality. —C. H. Spurgeon, Hindrances to Prayer

When you know that God hears your prayers, it seems silly to hold yourself back from doing it as often as possible. Constant prayer keeps your heart attuned to the voice of the Lord. It keeps your attention on what he has done, is doing, and will do.

Let gratitude be a constant prayer. Let each breath you notice serve as a reminder that God's presence is as close as the air around you. Let every mindful moment be an opportunity to breathe in God's grace and breathe out a prayer of thanksgiving. He is close, he is powerful, and he is full of love. You can't exhaust his mercy, so lean into it as often as you remember: you are his child, and he is your good Father.

Take a few deep breaths, and give gratitude for each one to your gracious Maker.

SPIRITUAL FORCES

Our struggle is not against flesh and blood, but against the rulers, against the powers, against the world forces of this darkness, against the spiritual forces of wickedness in the heavenly places.

Ephesians 6:12 NASB

Christians fight best on their knees. Whatever good may be done is done and brought about by prayer.—Martin Luther, Table Talk

Prayer guides our spiritual weapons to where they can best be used. When we begin to dismiss the humanity of our neighbors and start to see them as the enemy, we have gone off track. Jesus spent his ministry showing the audacious love of God to those we might ridicule. This should challenge us! Prayer is a powerful way to engage the heart of God, and to refocus our energy on fighting against the things that come against God's kingdom.

Prayer is a place where we can fight for love to reign in our hearts and minds. It is where we can pour out our grief and rage against the injustices of this world. Let's refocus our energy on fighting the powers of darkness, not our neighbors.

When you are tempted to fight with someone over disagreements, pray instead.

THE LORD HEARS

The righteous cry out, and the Lord hears,
and rescues them from all their troubles.
Psalm 34:17 csb

Faith in a prayer-hearing God will make a prayer-loving Christian.
—Andrew Murray, With Christ in the School of Prayer

Prayer wouldn't mean much if there wasn't the assurance of God's listening ear on the other end. When we pray, our words do not land flat in the room around us. Our prayers are heard by the Lord.

You don't have to speak your prayers out loud for God to hear. You don't have to open your lips, but to turn your heart, your mind, and your thoughts toward him is enough to open the line of communication. 1 Samuel 16:7 assures us, "Humans see what is visible, but the Lord sees the heart." He also hears your heart. Take courage in prayer, and trust the faithful one who hears your cries, even the silent ones.

Thank God for hearing your heart prayers, and for answering them.

Connected to the Vine

"I am the vine, and you are the branches. If any remain in me and I remain in them, they produce much fruit. But without me they can do nothing."

John 15:5 NCV

If we bring forth any good fruit, it is not of our own growth, it comes from him, the true vine. —Thomas Watson, The Ten Commandments

When we stay connected to Jesus, his life flows in and through us. His mercy changes our hearts and minds. His grace strengthens our ability to live his love out. His peace pervades our bodies and settles our nerves. Every good thing that comes out of our submission to Christ is the power of Christ's love at work in our lives.

We remain connected to Christ through following his ways and being obedient to his commands. This is how we remain in his love. Our prayers are powered by our faith-filled actions, and our actions are powered by prayer. Let's partner our prayer with obedience. That is how we stay connected to the true vine.

Back up your prayers with active faith and obedience to God's love.

ON RECORD

You keep track of all my sorrows.
You have collected all my tears in your bottle.
You have recorded each one in your book.
PSALM 56:8 NLT

I believe God has heard my prayers. He will make it manifest in His own good time that He has heard me. I have recorded my petitions that when God has answered them, His name will be glorified.
—George Müller, Narratives

God keeps track of our prayers, but that doesn't mean we can't also keep a record. When we pray and ask God to help us, we enter the waiting between prayer and provision. It is easy to overlook God's goodness when the pressures of yesterday are erased by his grace. When we keep a record of our prayers, we can also store up a well of gratitude as he answers them.

This isn't a practice that you have to do in order for God to answer you. He is faithful, and that will never change. When you write down your requests and come back to them, you may find that he answered them in ways you couldn't have anticipated. You can give gratitude and glory for the specific ways he answers your prayers. He is good, and worthy to be praised. And your heart will grow in faith as you witness his faithfulness.

Keep a log of your prayer requests. Come back to them weekly or quarterly, and write down when and how they have been answered.

MOTIVATED BY LOVE

"By this all will know that you are My disciples, if you have love for one another."
JOHN 13:35 NKJV

If you get love into your soul, so that the grace of God may come down in answer to prayer, there will be no trouble about reaching the people. It is not by eloquent sermons that perishing souls are going to be reached; we need the power of God in order that the blessing may come down. —D. L. Moody, Prevailing Prayer

Love is no little thing in the kingdom of God. It is the very nature of God and the foundation of everything he does. When we downplay the importance of love in our own lives, we distance ourselves from the heart of God.

First Corinthians thirteen is known as the love chapter. It reminds us that love is one of the few things that will last throughout eternity. It was present at the beginning of all things, and it will remain when the earth passes away. If we do anything, but we lack love, it is an empty shell. Love is the great motivator. It was what moved the Father to send his Son. It was the power that brought Christ back from the dead and offers us saving grace. It is what matters most.

Pray for a greater revelation of God's love so you can live it out.

LIVING COMPASSION

Be kind and compassionate to one another, forgiving each other, just as in Christ God forgave you.

EPHESIANS 4:32 NIV

It is not how much we do, but how much we love.
—Thomas Watson, All Things for Good

If we would do anything for God, it must be to love without restraint. Love that chooses kindness in the face of oppression. Love that is compassionate where others are judgmental. Love that forgives rather than holds on to grudges. Love that changes us from the inside out.

It is not overboard to say that forgiveness is an act of love. It releases us from the bitter root of hatred, and it does as Christ does, offering grace instead of condemnation. Choosing to be kind and compassionate and forgiving others does not mean condoning the harm that's been done. Pray for the strength to forgive as Christ does, while also standing with him for justice. It is possible to live in the freedom of his love and to offer it to others.

Pray for the strength to be as kind, compassionate, and forgiving as Christ is with you.

LISTENING HEART

"If anyone loves me, he will keep my word, and my Father will love him, and we will come to him and make our home with him."
JOHN 14:23 ESV

Dear brethren, if we shut our ears to what Jesus tells us, we shall never have power in prayer, nor shall we enjoy intimate communion with the Well-beloved. —C. H. Spurgeon, Prayer and Spiritual Warfare

A listening heart is as important in prayer as one that speaks. Prayer is not a one-sided conversation. There is room to hear the voice of the Lord if we take the time to listen. His living love speaks through the Word, the power of his presence, and through the wisdom of creation. He is all around, and he is speaking. If we have ears to hear, we will hear the Living Word.

If we want to be close to the Lord, we need to get to know him. If we want to know the power of prayer, we need to know the one we are praying to. As we direct our love, our curiosity, and our attention to our Savior, he pours out his wisdom, power, and love right back.

Practice listening prayer today.

MERCIFUL GOD

Blessed be the God and Father of our Lord Jesus Christ. Because of his great mercy he has given us new birth into a living hope through the resurrection of Jesus Christ from the dead.

1 PETER 1:3 CSB

In all your prayers forget not to thank the Lord for his mercies.
—John Bunyan, A Discourse Touching Prayer

God's mercies are new every morning, and his love doesn't fail. That means every morning is a fresh opportunity to turn our gaze to the Lord's goodness and receive the fresh bread of his presence. His love will not fail us. Ever. Not yesterday, not today, and not tomorrow. It is new every morning.

When we remember the Lord's faithful presence each morning and turn to him in prayer, our hearts are grounded in his goodness. We don't have to search the world for him. We don't have to go to church to find him. He is near. He is here. Right now, in this very moment, full of mercy, grace, and kindness. Won't you thank him for his living hope?

Begin each morning thanking God for his mercy. What great hope you have in him.

UNITED WITH CHRIST

"The glory which You have given Me I also have given to them, so that they may be one, just as We are one; I in them and You in Me, that they may be perfected in unity, so that the world may know that You sent Me, and You loved them, just as You loved Me."

JOHN 17:22-23 NASB

The whole reason why we pray is to be united into the vision and contemplation of God to whom we pray.
—Julian of Norwich, Revelations of Divine Love

Prayer isn't throwing wishes against a wall and seeing what sticks. It is the connective tissue of relationship with the Creator of all things. We are meant to be united to Christ, just as he is united with the Father. We are living reflections of his love. The more we behold him, the more we become like him.

Prayer can unite your heart quickly to God. Let it be more than a channel of needs presented to him. Let it serve as a conduit of listening to his heart, as well. Union comes not by accident, but through connection. Unite your heart to God through prayer, and his nature will flow through the cracks of your life like water seeps through every opening it finds.

Pray to deepen your relationship with God, not just to get things from him.

LIVING PRAYER

Pray without ceasing
1 Thessalonians 5:17 NKJV

Whether we think of or speak to God; whether we act or suffer for him; all is prayer when we have no other object than his love, and the desire of pleasing him. —John Wesley, A Plain Account of Christian Perfection

Living with the intention of our hearts open before the Lord, longing to please him, our lives become a continual prayer. What more can be said?

Prayers are not only the petitions and praises we offer to God. They are the surrendered actions of our lives, the choice to humble ourselves rather than exalt our own name. The choice to serve our neighbor and feed the hungry. God's love shines brightly through the lives of those who are devoted to him and to his purposes. Those who live out his love, following the ways of Christ on the path he paved, are those who reveal the power of the fragrant offering of their prayerful lives.

Make your actions—your choices, interactions, and service—your expression of prayer today.

LIVE IN PEACE

Do your best to live in peace with everyone.
Romans 12:18 NCV

Accustom yourself gradually to carry Prayer into all your daily occupation—speak, act, work in peace, as if you were in prayer, as indeed you ought to be. —François Fénelon, Selections from Fénelon

In a chaotic world, it is possible to live in peace. Everything we do—from our jobs to our hobbies, to home life, to interacting with people—can reflect the power of God's peace at work in us.

Though we have trouble in this world, we have peace in him. This is the same peace spoken of in Philippians 4:6-7, "Pray and ask God for everything you need, always giving thanks. And God's peace, which is so great we cannot understand it, will keep your hearts and minds in Christ Jesus." Prayer is the pathway to God's peace.

Pray throughout your day. Notice the difference it makes in your sense of peace.

THY WILL BE DONE

"Father, if you are willing, please take this cup of suffering away from me. Yet I want your will to be done, not mine."
LUKE 22:42 NLT

Thy will be done, my Lord: and, if I ask anything that is not in accordance therewith, my inmost will is that thou wouldst be good enough to deny thy servant; I will take it as a true answer if thou refuse me, if I ask that which seemeth not good in thy sight.
—C. H. Spurgeon, The Throne of Grace

There is power in pouring our hearts out before the Lord with the truth of what we feel in the moment. When we push through to the next step, as Jesus did in the Garden of Gethsemane, we experience the peace and confidence of God's wisdom.

Don't hold your prayers back for fear that you don't know God's will in it. Pray your heart out, and then trust it to the Lord by loosening your grip. God knows what is best better than you do. You can trust his heart and his hand, for he is full of loving-kindness and mercy doesn't fail. He will never trick, manipulate, or humiliate you. Every no is a not this: something better. Trust him, even and especially when you don't understand. His nature doesn't change, and he sees everything with clarity and wisdom that you don't have.

End your prayers with Jesus' own words, "Yet I want your will to be done, not mine."

PRAYING FOR OTHERS

"I say to you, love your enemies, bless those who curse you, do good to those who hate you, and pray for those who spitefully use you and persecute you."
MATTHEW 5:44 NKJV

Talking to men for God is a great thing, but talking to God for men is greater still. —E. M. Bounds, Power Through Prayer

Prayer isn't just a personal practice. Our faith deepens as we bring others before the throne of grace. As we pray for those around us, let's not only pray for those we love and like. Let's also take Jesus' words to heart, and pray for our enemies.

The love of God transforms us from the inside out. As we do good to those who mistreat us, and we pray for those who despise us, we join our hearts with the heart of the Father. This kind of connection leaves little room for bitterness to grow. God is our defender and our advocate. He knows us through and through, and we don't have to defend ourselves. It is our highest responsibility to love others as Christ loves us. Prayer helps us ready our hearts to do just that.

Pray for the people who test your sense of patience and kindness.

GREAT EXPECTATIONS

My God will meet all your needs according to the riches of his glory in Christ Jesus.

Philippians 4:19 NIV

Think of what He can do, and how He delights to hear the prayers of His redeemed people. Think of your place and privilege in Christ, and expect great things! —Andrew Murray, With Christ in the School of Prayer

God is ready and able to meet our needs out of the abundance of his resources. Why would we keep our prayers limited when God is ready to exceed our expectations with his glorious goodness?

Whatever your expectations of God, may they rise up to meet his faithfulness. Don't hold back your needs from the one who formed you. He knows what you need before you ask (Matthew 6:8), and he delights in answering the prayers of his people (Jeremiah 33:3). There is nothing keeping you from the love of Christ today, so don't keep yourself from reaching out to the one who knows you best.

Pray with great expectation of God's goodness.

WAIT FOR THE LORD

I wait for the LORD, my soul waits,
and in his word I hope.
PSALM 130:5-6 ESV

He who would work with God must first wait on Him and wait for Him, and that all undue haste in such a matter is worse than waste.
—George Müller, Narratives

There is no rush today. There is no hurry in God's presence. His presence is peace, and his love expands rather than restricts us. There is freedom in God's grace, and we can know that deep sense of present generosity in our communion with him through prayer.

Wait for the Lord today. Wait on him. Put your hope in his Living Word, and trust his timing. Practice patience and even as you move about your day, keep your soul in a state of expectant waiting. Keep your heart alert for the Lord, and you will sense him when he moves. You will see his hand, hear his voice, and know his peace. Keep waiting as you live each day. Prayerful waiting is powerful.

Keep your heart open in prayerful waiting before the Lord today.

PRAYING THE PROMISES

The yes to all of God's promises is in Christ, and through Christ we say yes to the glory of God.

2 Corinthians 1:20 NCV

If we read the Word and do not pray, we may become puffed up with knowledge, without the love that buildeth up. If we pray without reading the Word, we shall be ignorant of the mind and will of God, and become mystical and fanatical, and liable to be blown about by every wind of doctrine. —D. L. Moody, Prevailing Prayer

One of the most powerful practices of prayer is partnering it with the Word of God. Praying Scripture gives us confidence to know that we are standing on the foundation of God's revealed wisdom.

Whether we use a psalm as the starting point, or a favorite promise of God in Scripture, we can partner our faith with God's faithfulness. Jesus Christ is the yes and amen of every promise of God. He is our living hope and our redeemer. He is the Living Word, and he is the fullness of God in human form. Let's join our hearts and prayers to his promises, and pray from the firm foundation of his love.

Pick a verse or passage to pray from today.

LISTENING IN LOVE

However, God has listened;
he has paid attention to the sound of my prayer.
Blessed be God!
He has not turned away my prayer
or turned his faithful love from me.
PSALM 66:19-20 CSB

Prayer delights God's ear; it melts His heart.
—Thomas Watson, The Lord's Prayer

We know communication is powerful. It's not only in the speaking, but also in the deep listening. How does it make you feel to know that God listens to the sound of your voice? Does it move you to realize he leans in faithful love toward you as you reach out to him?

God your Father is listening in love, really listening to what you say. Whether you have people in your life who take time to hear the nuances of your heart or not, you can be sure that God does. He cares about what's on your heart. Go ahead, pour your heart out to him. He loves to listen to you as long as you need. And he will respond to you; you can be sure of it.

Tell God what's on your heart.

In Jesus' Name

"If you ask Me anything in My name, I will do it."
John 14:14 nasb

Prayer is the slender nerve that moves the muscle of Omnipotence.
—C. H. Spurgeon, The Power of Prayer and the Prayer of Power

Jesus did not do anything without the Father's power working in and through him. Jesus assured his followers, "Believe me when I say that I am in the Father and the Father is in me…whoever believes in me will do the works I have been doing, and they will do even greater things" (John 14:11-12).

It is from this basis, of doing the will of Christ, that we ask him for anything and he promises to do it. When we walk in the ways of Christ, we walk in the power of God. When we move in compassion and generosity toward the poor, when we help those overlooked by others, when we live by love's law, we can ask in Jesus' name for all we need—for miracles, signs, and wonders—and we will have it.

Ask the Lord to move in power through your life as you follow his ways.

TRUSTWORTHY JESUS

Let us go right into the presence of God with sincere hearts fully trusting him. For our guilty consciences have been sprinkled with Christ's blood to make us clean, and our bodies have been washed with pure water.

Hebrews 10:22 NLT

My prayer life must be brought entirely under the control of Christ and his love. Then, for the first time, will prayer become what it really is, the natural and joyous breathing of the spiritual life, by which the heavenly atmosphere is inhaled and then exhaled in prayer.
—Andrew Murray, The Prayer Life

The power of Christ's saving grace frees us from guilt, shame, and fear. We don't have to wonder whether he accepts us. He lovingly embraces us as his own as we put our faith in him. Our prayer lives can know this powerful purity too. As we yield our lives to the love of Christ, our hearts overflow with praise and thanks.

Put your wholehearted trust in the Savior today. Go right into his presence with the confidence of a dearly loved child. You don't have to hesitate at the doorway of his presence. He welcomes you with open arms. Come in, receive his grace, and let his joy fill you and fuel your prayers.

Remember who you are in Christ, and enter his courts with praise.

THIS I KNOW

When I cry out to You,
Then my enemies will turn back;
This I know, because God is for me.
PSALM 56:9 NKJV

Seek by prayer to move the Arm that moves the world.
—D. L. Moody, Prevailing Prayer

We cannot control what others choose. We can only direct our own hearts and actions. Still, through prayer, we call on the one who can do far greater things than we can imagine. Though we cannot dictate the tide of battle, the Lord can miraculously move on our behalf. The psalmist cried out to the Lord, and then the tide of battle turned in his favor (Psalm 56).

God is our defender, protector, and Savior. When we cry out to him, he moves. It may not always happen as we expect, but we can be sure he is at work in the details. God's heart is moved by the prayers of his people. Let's not neglect the power of prayer "to move the Arm that moves the world."

Are you worried about something? Pray for God's intervention.

PRAYERFUL ACTION

"Watch and pray so that you will not fall into temptation. The spirit is willing, but the flesh is weak."
MATTHEW 26:41 NIV

You can do more than pray after you've prayed, but you cannot do more than pray until you have prayed. —S.D. Gordon, Quiet Talks on Prayer

If we want to partner with the Lord, we cannot neglect prayer. Prayer must be the basis of our actions, for God is the one who strengthens, guides, and moves through us. When prayer becomes a natural rhythm to our day, we keep the lines of communication between us and God open. This is a powerful and peaceful way to live.

Temptation to compromise will come, and that's why it's important to remain watchful and prayerful. When we do make mistakes, let us be quick to repent and restore our hearts to God. He knows us, and he doesn't expect perfection from us. He takes our weak willingness and moves with the empowering grace of his presence.

Pray before you act, inviting God to guide you.

FOUNDATION OF FAITH

"What must we do, to be doing the works of God?" Jesus answered them, "This is the work of God, that you believe in him whom he has sent."

JOHN 6:28-29 ESV

Prayer in its legitimate possibilities goes out on God Himself. Prayer goes out with faith not only in the promise of God, but faith in God Himself, and in God's ability to do. Prayer goes out not on the promise merely, but "obtains promises," and creates promises.
—E. M. Bounds, The Possibilities of Prayer

To be doing the works of God, we must first have a foundation of faith. We put our faith in Christ as the Son of God and Savior of our souls, and all else comes from the strength of standing upon his work.

God's work is greater than ours. Faith is accessible. It is the foundation, and from that place everything else flows. The greatest work of God is his saving grace. He does this in our hearts, minds, and lives, and we are freed from fear, sin, shame, and death. There is eternal hope in the power of his love, and we get to live in it!

Meditate on the power of God's saving grace through Christ.

MOTIVATED BY LOVE

Our only goal is to please God whether we live here or there.
2 Corinthians 5:9 NCV

Whether we think of, or speak to, God, whether we act or suffer for him, all is prayer, when we have no other object than his love, and the desire of pleasing him. —John Wesley, A Plain Account of Christian Perfection

When we are motivated by the desire to please the Lord and to live by pouring out the overflow of his love, everything we do becomes a living prayer. First thing's first. Instead of focusing on what we can do for him, let's focus our attention on what he has already done for us. As the awareness of his goodness and mercy floods our soul, let's give him gratitude.

Let everything you do today reflect the gratitude you feel toward the Savior. He has done great things, and he will continue to do them. He has saved you, and he is delivering you still. Praise him through your loving surrender and live out his love as you receive it.

Let your actions be your prayerful sacrifice today.

FRIENDSHIP WITH GOD

There is a friend who stays closer than a brother.
Proverbs 18:24 CSB

Prayer is nothing else than being on terms of friendship with God.
—St. Teresa of Ávila, The Life of Teresa of Jesus

How often do you talk to your friends? You probably don't go weeks without a conversation. Close proximity surely helps in staying up to date with what's going on in each other's lives. Now, think about how often you pray.

Do you consider Jesus a friend? If that's not the role he's played in your life, it can be life-changing to know him in this deeper way. He is closer than a brother, always available, and he doesn't require explanations that others might. He knows you through and through, and he is a faithful help in times of trouble. He is always there. Start talking to him like you would a friend, and a friend he surely will become.

Pray to God as if you were talking to a close friend.

EVEN SO

This is real love—not that we loved God, but that he loved us and sent his Son as a sacrifice to take away our sins.

1 JOHN 4:10 NLT

If I feel myself disinclined to pray, then is the time when I need to pray more than ever.
—C. H. Spurgeon, Comfort for Those Whose Prayers are Feeble

You don't have to be in the mood to pray to do it. In fact, you might need prayer the most in those moments. In an intentional turning of your heart to the Lord, you stand upon the power of his love. He loves you first, foremost, and fully. Even when you can't access that love in yourself, his supply has not run dry.

God doesn't require you to be in a good mood to come before him. You don't have to pretend to be anything that you aren't. Bring him your full and true self. Simply choose to pray. Even if it is a short, "Help, Lord." He can read between the lines. He will answer you, and you can trust that when he does, it will be full of the power of his love.

No matter your mood, bring God your authentic prayers.

BELIEF IN ACTION

Do you see that faith was working together with his works, and by works faith was made perfect? And the Scripture was fulfilled which says, "Abraham believed God, and it was accounted to him for righteousness."

JAMES 2:22-23 NKJV

Prayer is never an acceptable substitute for obedience. The sovereign Lord accepts no offering from His creatures that is not accompanied by obedience. To pray for revival while ignoring or actually flouting the plain precept laid down in the Scriptures is to waste a lot of words and get nothing for our trouble. —A. W. Tozer, Paths to Power

Faith moves our prayers, but it shouldn't end there. After we pray for God's help, we move in the confident assurance of his faithfulness. If we truly believe God is who he says he is, our actions will reflect it.

Go ahead and pour out your prayers to the Lord. Open your heart to him. And then live like you trust him. Live like you believe that his promises are sure. Abraham trusted God's word over his life, and he left his home in obedience to that promise. Prayer is part of the equation. Obedience is the other.

Don't just pray for God's help today. Follow his lead, and trust him to provide.

PRIVATE PRAYER

"When you pray, go into your room, close the door and pray to your Father, who is unseen. Then your Father, who sees what is done in secret, will reward you."

Matthew 6:6 NIV

Prayer—secret fervent believing prayer—lies at the root of all personal godliness. —E. M. Bounds, Power Through Prayer

Godliness begins in the heart behind closed doors where no one else sees. It is a posture of surrender before the Lord in the secret place. If we want to live godly lives, it begins in the personal place of prayerful submission.

Prioritizing our personal prayer time is a good way to set the rest of our day up for success. Success doesn't equate to wealth, ease, or power. It equates with peace, love, and joy: the fruits of God's Spirit at work within us. God recognizes the posture of our hearts, and he honors the humble. As we humble ourselves before him, he strengthens us by his grace, his presence, and his power.

Spend time in the secret place of prayer today.

IT'S NO TROUBLE

Humble yourselves, therefore, under the mighty hand of God so that at the proper time he may exalt you, casting all your anxieties on him, because he cares for you.

1 PETER 5:6-7 ESV

We sometimes fear to bring our troubles to God, because they must seem small to Him who sitteth on the circle of the earth. But if they are large enough to vex and endanger our welfare, they are large enough to touch His heart of love. —R. A. Torrey, How to Pray

What troubles you is of no small matter to your heavenly Father. Bring him every anxiety, every care, every question, and lay it down before him. He exalts the humble, and he gives strength to the weary.

You don't have to struggle on your own. You don't have to figure out your problems or fix the chaos of the world. You can only do so much, and it's too weighty of a responsibility. God doesn't expect you to know what you don't know. He sees clearly, and he has wisdom for your confusion, peace for your worried heart, and a plan to guide you through it all.

Cast your cares on the Lord, knowing he cares for you. Don't withhold a thing.

DIRECTED HOPE

Rest in God alone, my soul,
for my hope comes from him.
PSALM 62:5 CSB

True prayer is an approach of the soul by the Spirit of God to the throne of God. It is not the utterance of words, it is not alone the feeling of desires, but it is the advance of the desires to God, the spiritual approach of our nature towards the Lord our God.
—C. H. Spurgeon, The Throne of Grace

Prayer is not only words reaching the listening ear of God. Our hearts are brought before the Lord, turning our inner attention to his present nearness through his Spirit. There is a divine exchange of peace, hope, and joy as we lay down our burdens and present ourselves as his willing children, ready to hear his voice and move in responsive obedience.

God's requirements of us are not too much, and we will discover just how easy he is to please as we get to know him more through prayer, fellowship, and his Word. We bring our desires to God. He sees, he knows, he responds. We have only to take his outstretched hand and follow him as he leads us in loving wisdom.

Direct your soul toward the Lord's presence and the rest he offers.

GREAT THINGS

Confess your sins to each other and pray for each other so God can heal you. When a believing person prays, great things happen.
James 5:16 NCV

None can believe how powerful prayer is, and what it is able to effect, but those who have learned it by experience. It is a great matter when in extreme need to take hold on prayer. I know, whenever I have prayed earnestly, that I have been amply heard, and have obtained more than I prayed for. God indeed sometimes delayed, but at last He came. —Martin Luther, Table Talk

God responds to our heartfelt prayers. He is faithful to rescue those in trouble. He is close to the brokenhearted, and he heals their wounds. There is no trouble so great that God cannot reach you in it. There is no chasm so wide that he will not close the distance in a moment's notice. He is with you in your struggles, and he will not leave you alone.

When extreme need is felt, take hold of prayer. It directs your need to the faithfulness of the Creator of all things. He has not failed, and he will not fail you.

How has God answered your prayers of need before?

FILLED WITH LOVE

I love the Lord, because He hears
My voice and my pleas.
Because He has inclined His ear to me,
Therefore I will call upon Him as long as I live.
Psalm 116:1-2 NASB

In souls filled with love, the desire to please God is continual prayer.
—John Wesley, A Plain Account of Christian Perfection

God's kindness draws us to himself. It is his love that leads us to repentance. When we respond to God's love, we cannot help but be filled with its life-giving waters. Our response echoes the love of God's heart.

Call upon the Lord. Keep praying. The fire of love keeps burning in the soul that is in constant communion with its Creator. Remember the passion you felt at first when you came to the Lord and return to the purity of that love. Reach toward the Lord in love, and you will be filled with even more of his kindness.

Offer the love you have to God, and watch as he fills the reservoir of your soul with an even greater portion.

SPIRIT LED

You are not controlled by your sinful nature. You are controlled by the Spirit if you have the Spirit of God living in you.
ROMANS 8:9 NLT

The true spirit of prayer is no other than God's own Spirit dwelling in the hearts of the saints. And as this spirit comes from God, so doth it naturally tend to God in holy breathings and pantings. It naturally leads to God, to converse with him by prayer.
—Jonathan Edwards, Hypocrites Deficient in the Duty of Prayer

When we submit our lives to Christ, putting our faith in him as the Son of God, there is nothing that separates us from his presence. Nothing! The Spirit makes his home in the heart of every believer. You don't have to go searching outside of yourself, and you don't have to worry about missing the Spirit's fellowship. If you are in Christ, Christ is in you.

Let the Spirit lead you in prayer especially when you're not sure what to pray. He will intercede for you. Take a deep breath, turn your heart to God, and allow yourself to experience Spirit-to-spirit fellowship.

Do you know that the Spirit of God lives in you?

QUENCH YOUR THIRST

As the deer pants for the water brooks,
So pants my soul for You, O God.
My soul thirsts for God, for the living God.
When shall I come and appear before God?
Psalm 42:1-2 NKJV

Some people pray just to pray and some people pray to know God.
—Andrew Murray, With Christ in the School of Prayer

Jesus said in John 4:14, “Whoever drinks of the water that I shall give him will never thirst. But the water that I shall give him will become in him a fountain of water springing up into everlasting life.” When your soul thirsts for God, you can be sure that you will be satisfied by Christ himself!

When you pray, press in to know the one who calls you in kindness. There is more goodness, truth, peace, and joy in him than you can imagine. His life-giving waters satisfy the parched soul, and he refreshes the weak with his powerful grace.

Pray, not just to tell God what you need, but to know him more.

MORNING JOY

Restore to me the joy of your salvation
and grant me a willing spirit, to sustain me.
Psalm 51:12 NIV

The first great and primary business to which I ought to attend every day is to have my soul happy in the Lord. —George Müller, Narratives

Every morning is an opportunity to start fresh in the mercy of God. Before we set foot out of bed, before we start our day, let us practice turning our hearts to the Lord. It doesn't matter if we enjoy the morning or not, there is an opportunity to feast on the joy of the Lord as we awaken our hearts in praise.

What would it do for your prayer life to start your day with gratitude? It could turn hesitation to joy-fueled thanks. No matter how the rest of your day goes, begin it in the secret place with the Lord where there is hope, peace, love, and joy to feed your soul. Rejoice in the Lord, for he is near.

Begin your mornings with thanking the Lord for three things and praise him for his goodness.

SHINING FACE

The LORD bless you and keep you;
the LORD make his face to shine upon you
and be gracious to you;
the LORD lift up his countenance upon you
and give you peace.
NUMBERS 6:24-26 ESV

So when we get really into communion with God, He lifts up His countenance upon us; and instead of our having gloomy looks, our faces will shine, because God has heard and answered our prayers. Jesus. —D. L. Moody, Prevailing Prayer

You can tell when someone has been spending time in the sunshine. The warmth of the sun's rays sinks into their skin and colors their cheeks. In the same way, you can tell when someone has been in the presence of the Son. Their face shines with the peace of God's presence.

Receive the blessing of today's prayer over your heart, mind, and body. May your face shine brightly with the peace that passes all understanding as you spend time in God's presence.

Turn your heart toward the Lord and soak in the light of his love like you would the rays of the sun.

FULLNESS OF GOD

Christ's love is greater than anyone can ever know, but I pray that you will be able to know that love. Then you can be filled with the fullness of God.

Ephesians 3:19 NCV

Herein lies the whole secret of a real Christian life, a life of liberty and joy and power and fullness. To have as one's ever-present Friend, and to be conscious that one has as his ever-present Friend, the Holy Spirit and to surrender one's life in all its departments entirely to His control, this is true Christian living.
—R. A. Torrey, The Person and Work of The Holy Spirit

The power of Christ isn't a theory to the believer. It is the lived experience of his love setting us free from shame, healing our wounds, and settling our hearts in peace. There is more goodness in his fellowship than we have yet tasted!

If we want to truly know the fullness of God, we must know the lengths of his love. His love is ever-expanding, never diminishing, and creates breakthroughs of powerful peace. Where we have a deficit of understanding, peace, or joy, there is more of God to fill those spaces with his gracious presence.

Surrender your weakness to God and ask him to fill the cracks of your understanding with his abundant love.

PRESENT PORTION

"I am the bread of life," Jesus told them. "No one who comes to me will ever be hungry, and no one who believes in me will ever be thirsty again."

JOHN 6:35 CSB

True prayers are born of present trials and present needs. Bread for today is bread enough. Bread given for today is the strongest sort of pledge that there will be bread tomorrow. Victory today is the assurance of victory tomorrow. —E. M. Bounds, The Necessity of Prayer

Our needs can either drive us crazy or drive us to the great provider. Worry wants to take us out of the present moment into the unknowns of tomorrow. How can we know our needs will be met tomorrow? We cannot know the exact details, but that is not what trust is. Trust requires unknown.

God is with us here. He is with us now. His present portion—our daily bread—is enough. When we learn to live in that, we experience greater peace, clarity, and closeness to the one who holds our hearts.

When you begin to worry about tomorrow, redirect your attention to God's grace and provision.

STRAIGHT TO THE POINT

"When you are praying, do not use thoughtless repetition as the Gentiles do, for they think that they will be heard because of their many words."

MATTHEW 6:7 NASB

Little of the Word with little prayer is death to the spiritual life. Much of the Word with little prayer gives a sickly life. Much prayer with little of the Word gives more life, but without steadfastness. A full measure of the Word and prayer each day gives healthy and powerful life. —Andrew Murray, The Prayer Life

There's nothing wrong with telling God what's on your heart. But don't think it's the exactness or way you say something that gets him to listen and respond. God isn't impressed by grandiose speeches. He's not concerned with how you say something; rather that it comes from a heart that is true.

If you want your prayer life to be strengthened, knowing the Word is incredibly important. As your understanding of the wisdom of God deepens, so will your prayers.

Spend time in the Word, and pray from that place.

PRECIOUS TREASURE

Wisdom is more profitable than silver,
and her wages are better than gold.
Wisdom is more precious than rubies;
nothing you desire can compare with her.
Proverbs 3:14-15 NLT

The spirit of prayer is more precious than treasures of gold and silver.
—John Bunyan, Mr. John Bunyan's Dying Sayings

Many put their confidence in the things of this world. They build their treasures on earth, thinking it can guarantee their security. There is nothing wrong with being wise about our resources, but none of it is a guarantee of what we will have tomorrow. It is much better to pursue the heavenly treasures of God's kingdom as we align our hearts and lives in Christ's love.

The ways of God are not the ways of men; they are better. He is better. Psalm 20:7 says, "Some nations boast of their chariots and horses, but we boast in the name of the Lord our God." It is much better to rely on God than to rely on the power, wealth, and influence of imperfect people.

Seek the Lord's favor, his help, and his leadership through prayer.

ALWAYS PRAYING

O LORD, You have searched me and known me.
You know my sitting down and my rising up;
You understand my thought afar off.
You comprehend my path and my lying down,
And are acquainted with all my ways.
PSALM 139:1-3 NKJV

I live in the spirit of prayer. I pray as I walk about, when I lie down and when I rise up. And the answers are always coming.
—George Müller, An Hour with George Müller

The spirit of prayer is an attitude—a posture—of open-heartedness before the Lord. As we walk, we breathe thanks for the beauty around us. As we stand, we remember that our bodies are not always strong, but God's presence is. When we lie down, we offer God every burden, concern, and person who is struggling around us. Everything can be fuel for prayer when our hearts remain active in the spirit of prayer.

Prayer doesn't have to be formal to make a difference. Learn to practice it throughout your day by pairing it with something you already do. When you brush your teeth, pray for your family. When you drive, pray for the people around you. When you walk, use it to praise God for his thoughtfulness. Make prayer a lifestyle rather than an isolated act.

Use cues around you as reminders to pray.

BELIEVING PRAYER

"I tell you, whatever you ask for in prayer, believe that you have received it, and it will be yours."
Mark 11:24 NIV

All through the Scriptures you will find that when believing prayer went up to God, the answer came down. —D. L. Moody, Prevailing Prayer

There is power in the faith-filled prayer. Where does our faith come from? Does it not come from the seeds planted in us by God himself? Ephesians 2:8 reminds us, "It is by grace you have been saved, through faith—and this is not form yourselves, it is the gift of God." Gracious faith, any amount we have, was first deposited in us by the Lord.

We can nurture and tend to the seeds of faith by bringing our prayers to the Lord, walking in obedience to his wisdom, and living out his love. Even faith as small as a mustard seed has power to move mountains, so let's not keep our little bits of faith hoarded away for another day. Let's ask in faith, believing the one who hears us is ready to respond, and trust him to do just that.

Rather than worrying about the amount of faith you have, pray with confidence and trust the one who created you to come through for you.

RESTORATIVE POWER

I will greatly rejoice in the Lord;
my soul shall exult in my God,
for he has clothed me with the garments of salvation;
he has covered me with the robe of righteousness.
Isaiah 61:10 ESV

Upon our turning to God, we have more restored to us in Christ than ever was lost in Adam. God says to the repenting soul, "I will clothe you with the robe of righteousness; I will enrich you with the jewels and graces of my Spirit. I will bestow my love upon you! I will give you a kingdom! Son, all I have is yours!"
—Thomas Watson, The Doctrine of Repentance

Jesus is our Redeemer. He doesn't only redeem our souls from death, but he also brings restoration to various parts of our lives. We can trust the one who clothes his people with the robe of righteousness to care for us, deliver us, and restore what was lost along the way. He really is that good!

There are treasures to be discovered in the life of the Spirit. There is more goodness ahead. There isn't a thing we leave behind that will not be restored in the perfect love of Christ in the fullness of his kingdom. What is lost will be found, and it will be sweeter than we can anticipate.

Ask God to reveal his restorative power to you today.

SIMPLY ASK

"Ask of me, and I will make the nations your inheritance
and the ends of the earth your possession."
Psalm 2:8 CSB

God does nothing but in answer to prayer.
—John Wesley, A Plain Account of Christian Perfection

God moves, and the earth trembles. God speaks, and the winds and waves respond. Do you know what is incredible? We don't have to wait for God to move to respond. We get to come before him as his children and ask for what we need. We get to ask for the desires of our hearts, and God will respond in ways that are best for us.

The ends of the earth are Christ's inheritance; we are his inheritance. The people of this world are God's greatest treasures. Let's not withhold our asking, and while we're at it, let's trust God to answer. God loves to delight his children, and when we know the power of his true and loving nature, we trust him with the details. He is God, he is good, and he is listening.

Take your prayers to your Father and remember you are free to ask for what's on your heart. Listen for his response.

ALL SUFFICIENT

"Every animal of the forest is already mine.
The cattle on a thousand hills are mine.
I know every bird on the mountains,
and every living thing in the fields is mine."
PSALM 50:10-11 NCV

The greatest need of our age and of every age, the greatest need of every human heart, is to know the resources and sufficiency of God.
—A.B. Simpson, When God Steps In

God owns the cattle on a thousand hills. All that is exists because of God. He isn't limited in resources; he created everything in the earth. You may not know how your needs will be met, but God's already got the provision. Don't doubt his goodness, for he is your faithful Father.

Have you known God's provision at other times in your life? Let them serve as reminders of his faithfulness. Thank him again and trust him to do what he so easily does. His timing may not be yours, and his ways may astonish you at times, but he is always faithful. He will come through for you when you need him.

Remember the greatness of God as you bring him your needs and trust him to follow-through in faithful provision.

STANDING ON THE PROMISES

The Lord is good,
A stronghold in the day of trouble,
And He knows those who take refuge in Him.
Nahum 1:7 NASB

If I am to have faith when I pray, I must find some promise in the Word of God to rest my faith on. —R. A. Torrey, How to Pray

The old hymn says, "Standing on the promises that cannot fail, when the howling storms of doubt and fear assail, by the living Word of God I shall prevail, standing on the promises of God."

When you stand on the foundation of God's Word in prayer, you have firm footing. Though the winds of uncertainty blow, God's faithfulness remains the rock beneath your feet. May you know the Lord's goodness, his assuring presence and powerful peace as you pray right back to him. There is nothing you face that hasn't already been faced by those who have gone before. Look through the pages of Scripture and you will find incredibly ordinary people made extraordinary for their trust in their faithful God.

Pair your prayers with the promises of God in Scripture.

DEEP COMMUNION

The Holy Spirit helps us in our weakness. For example, we don't know what God wants us to pray for. But the Holy Spirit prays for us with groanings that cannot be expressed in words.
ROMANS 8:26 NLT

True prayer is not a mere mental exercise, nor a vocal performance, but it is deeper far than that—it is spiritual commerce with the Creator of heaven and earth. —C. H. Spurgeon, The Throne of Grace

Prayer is not just what comes out of our lips directed toward God. It isn't even only the expressions of our hearts. Through the Spirit's fellowship, it is a deep, soul-level communion with the King of kings.

The Holy Spirit intercedes for us when we have no words. He expresses what we don't know how and relays it to the Father. There is power in the companionship of the Spirit. He can offer the truth of what is in us even when we don't recognize it. How intricately we are known, and how thoughtfully we are brought into communion with our great God.

Ask the Spirit to take over when you don't have the words to pray.

LONGING FOR THE LORD

My soul longs, yes, even faints
For the courts of the Lord;
My heart and my flesh cry out for the living God.
Psalm 84:2 NKJV

The ministry of prayer, if it be anything worthy of the name, is a ministry of ardor, a ministry of unwearied and intense longing after God and after his holiness. —E. M. Bounds, The Essentials of Prayer

God's passionate pursuit of us in love is remarkable. Our own longing grows as we discover how wonderful, patient, kind, and generous he is. When we feel that longing, let's not put it on a shelf to pursue another day. Let's embrace the hunger of our heart by connecting with the Lord in prayer.

Prayerful praise is the most natural extension of our longing for the Lord. Psalm 84 is a declaration of the psalmist's hunger. "For a day in Your courts is better than a thousand [elsewhere]" (v. 10). What is God's love like to you? How would you describe his goodness? Let your longing lead you in honest praise, and pour your heart out to your Creator.

Read through Psalm 84 and make it your personal prayer today.

SECRET OF CONTENTMENT

I know what it is to be in need, and I know what it is to have plenty. I have learned the secret of being content in any and every situation, whether well fed or hungry, whether living in plenty or in want.

PHILIPPIANS 4:12 NIV

Prayer is a surge of the heart, it is a simple look turned toward heaven, it is a cry of recognition and of love, embracing both trial and joy.
—St. Therese of Lisieux, Story of a Soul

When we let our circumstances dictate our peace or contentment, we guarantee that we will flounder in hard times. The truth is this: we will have good seasons of plenty, and we will have harsh seasons of scarcity. How do we keep our hearts rooted in trust no matter what's going on around us?

Paul found the secret of being content in every situation no matter the depth of his need or the abundance of his resources. It was simple for him, and it remains simple for us. "I can do all this through him who gives me strength." It is Christ's grace that empowers us with strength to persevere in hard times. It is his love that brings peace to our hearts, minds, and bodies—no matter the circumstance.

Remember Paul's statement, and let it become your own prayer.

CONFIDENT TRUST

He is not afraid of bad news;
his heart is firm, trusting in the Lord.
Psalm 112:7 ESV

God's command to "pray without ceasing" is founded on the necessity we have of His grace to preserve the life of God in the soul, which can no more subsist one moment without it, than the body can without air.
—John Wesley, A Plain Account of Christian Perfection

Bad news is inevitable. None of us gets an easy life without trouble. We are all touched by grief, loss, and pain—all of us! To deny this is to resist reality, and it is to keep ourselves at a distance from God's gracious comfort. He is near to the brokenhearted. He saves those whose spirits are crushed.

What do we do with bad news when it comes? Do we get busy and try to fix it? Do we pretend it's not happening? Do we turn to our support systems? Whatever we do in those first few minutes responding, let's not stay there. Let us bring our cares to the cross of Christ and lay them there. God is not surprised by the things that throw us off. He remains faithful and true.

Pray for a heart that trusts God in every circumstance.

ETERNAL TREASURES

"Store your treasures in heaven where they cannot be destroyed by moths or rust and where thieves cannot break in and steal them. Your heart will be where your treasure is."
MATTHEW 6:20-21 NCV

Laying up treasures in heaven will draw the heart heavenward.
—George Müller, Narratives

What does Jesus mean when he says that we should store our treasures in heaven? What he's pointing to is that money and wealth don't last. We can't take our possessions with us when we leave this earth, so why pour most of our energy into obtaining and keeping those things? A spirit of generosity keeps us close to God.

The treasures of God's kingdom look like justice, doing good to others, and helping those in need. They are the patience and kindness of God's love. They are acts of generosity and selflessness. They are communal acts of connection that build others up rather than tear them down. It all falls under the law of God's love. If that is your standard, you cannot go wrong.

What kinds of treasures are you storing up?

IMMEASURABLY MORE

Now to him who is able to do above and beyond all that we ask or think according to the power that works in us.
Ephesians 3:20 CSB

Prayer is God's plan to supply man's great and continuous need with God's great and continuous abundance.
—E. M. Bounds, Power Through Prayer

Just because God can do more than we ask of him, does this mean we should refrain from asking? By no means! Prayer moves God's heart, and he is delighted to respond in ways that go above and beyond what we meant when we asked. His resources are abundant, and there isn't a moment when this isn't true.

Our needs are ongoing because of the nature of humanity. We may have eaten a large meal yesterday, but does that mean we won't have to eat for another week? No, every day we need sustenance. Our spirits do, too. What does your soul need today? Ask the Father and thank him for his generous provision.

God delights in meeting your needs, so don't hesitate to ask him for what you need today.

ALONE WITH GOD

It was at this time that He went off to the mountain to pray, and He spent the whole night in prayer with God.
Luke 6:12 nasb

If we would continuously know the power of God we should go often alone with Him, at the close of each day at least, and ask Him to show us if any sin, anything displeasing in His sight, has crept in that day, and if He shows us that there has, we should confess it and put it away then and there. —R. A. Torrey, The Baptism with the Holy Spirit

Jesus often went off on his own to pray. If he, the Son of God, needed time alone with God in prayer, how much more do we? Let's follow the example of Christ and take time with him. It might not be an all-night affair, but let us at least take a few minutes to be alone each evening.

The practice of asking God to reveal if there is anything within us that needs to be aligned with his love is a powerful one. We can get caught up in the busyness of the demands of the day, but God wants us to learn to rest and recalibrate in his presence. Prayer gets us there.

Take some time in your prayer time to ask God to reveal if there is anything you need to confess and change.

TRUST IN THE WAITING

"This is our God!
We trusted in him, and he saved us!
This is the Lord, in whom we trusted.
Let us rejoice in the salvation he brings!"
Isaiah 25:9 NLT

Perhaps it takes a purer faith to praise God for unrealized blessings than for those we once enjoyed or those we enjoy now.
—A. W. Tozer, The Root of Righteousness

Trust is not needed in certainty. It is required in the liminal spaces and in the unknowns. We do not base our trust of God on knowing how everything will go; the details have yet to be worked out. We base our trust in the character of God.

Faith is required in many areas of life. Especially when the promises we await seem delayed. We don't know the timing of fulfilment, but we can trust his presence in the process. He takes care of us—he is with us—in each moment. Fellowship with God is our greatest gift in the waiting, and it teaches our hearts how to hold hope, peace, and joy in the waiting seasons.

What can you trust the Lord with today?

OUR HELPER

We may boldly say:
"The Lord is my helper;
I will not fear.
What can man do to me?"
Hebrews 13:6 NKJV

Be assured, if you walk with Him and look to Him, and expect help from Him, He will never fail you. —George Müller, Narratives

God is our ever-present help in times of trouble. He is our constant friend. We feel the need of God's help more desperately when we cannot see the way through. He is there as a loving shepherd and wise counselor. He will not lead us astray, and he will not leave us alone.

If all we have today is God's presence, it is more than enough. Let us not look at the lives of others and wonder why they have more than we do. Let's not equate our worth with resources, for God has said that he will take care of his people. He does not love anyone more than another. He loves you as you are—fully. Look to him, for he will continue to take care of you.

Pray for the grace to accept what God has given without comparing it to anyone else.

Inner Confidence

This is the confidence we have in approaching God: that if we ask anything according to his will, he hears us.
1 John 5:14 niv

My experience is that those who pray most in their closets generally make short prayers in public. —D. L. Moody, Prevailing Prayer

The inner confidence for bold prayers does not come from striving or from imitating others. It comes from a solid foundation of fellowship with the Lord behind closed doors. The more we cultivate our private prayer lives, the more sure we can be in our public prayers.

Think of it this way. A parent trains their child in the way they should go, and they also teach them what to expect of them. A generous parent leads by example. If we are out in public and come across someone who needs help and we know that we have our parent's blessing, we will do all we can to help them. The more we know what the Father is like, the more confidently we can walk in his authority.

Spend time in prayer to know God and what he is like.

PERSEVERANCE

I keep trying to reach the goal and get the prize for which God called me through Christ to the life above.
PHILIPPIANS 3:14 NCV

Storm the throne of grace and persevere therein, and mercy will come down. —John Wesley, Letter to Mrs. Bennis

If we give up easily in our pursuit of God, we miss out on the wonderful mysteries of his goodness. He is kind, faithful, and just. He has love to lavish on us each day. Our spirits strengthen in his presence, and our minds become clearer in the wisdom of his Word.

Pursuing the Lord in prayer will not always feel easy. There will be times when the practice brings us before him and we persevere in that place, past the blocks of doubt, discouragement, or fear. There is breakthrough for us when we do. We can be sure that God will meet us with powerful peace, glorious grace, and marvelous mercy as we push through. As we keep showing up, so does he, and he will not leave us thirsty. He offers the living waters of his presence to satisfy our souls.

Persevere in prayer when you'd rather give up and listen for God's voice.

STAY HUMBLE

Humble yourselves before the Lord, and he will exalt you.
James 4:10 CSB

He who loves with humility and prays fervently, will be heard by God; he who seeks God in prayer and in His service, will surely find Him. —Thomas à Kempis, The Imitation of Christ

Humble love leads to powerful prayers. God is able to lead the open heart, and the curious mind is ready to put wisdom into practice. When we think we already have the answer, when we let pride keep us from growing, we limit what we allow God to do in our lives.

If we want to grow in understanding, we have to humble ourselves. We have to admit that we don't know it all and look to the Lord for his wise leadership. He really is better than the best of men, and he never manipulates us, tricks us, or does things for selfish purposes. His love is ever-expanding, and as we humble ourselves, we make room to experience greater measures of it.

How can you humble yourself before the Lord today?

ALL IS POSSIBLE

"Nothing will be impossible with God."
Luke 1:37 ESV

All that God is, and all that God has, is at the disposal of prayer. Prayer can do anything that God can do, and as God can do everything, prayer is omnipotent.
—R. A. Torrey, The Power of Prayer and the Prayer of Power

Nothing is impossible for God. The Creator of all things can do whatever he wishes with what he has made. And yet, it is prayer that moves his heart. What a powerful privilege we have to come before him and petition him!

Mark 9:23, echoing what today's verse says, declares, "All things are possible for one who believes." These are Jesus' own words. If nothing is impossible with God, and all things are possible for one who believes, what is holding us back? What is keeping us from praying big, bold, authentic prayers to the one who is able to do more than we can imagine?

Let your prayers be based upon God's ability, not the status quo.

GOD'S WORK

"The Helper, the Holy Spirit whom the Father will send in My name, He will teach you all things, and remind you of all that I said to you."

John 14:26 NASB

Our spirit within us, begotten by the Holy Ghost at our regeneration, discerns the Great Spirit, communes with him, prefers to him its requests, and receives from him answers of peace. It is a spiritual business from beginning to end; and its aim and object end not with man, but reach to God himself. —C. H. Spurgeon, The Throne of Grace

We take our hunger to God, and he fills us. We bring our needs to the Lord, and he meets them. The Spirit of God moves first within us to draw us to the Lord. This is what he did in the beginning, and we can trust that he continues to move mysteriously to bring us closer.

The Holy Spirit is our teacher, our counselor, and our wise guide. We don't have to rely on our memories or understanding. If we will continue to go to the Lord and follow his leadership, we will know the power of God's Spirit filling us with what we need right when we need it.

Pray for the Spirit to teach you and instruct you in what you need today.

A SHARED LOAD

Share each other's burdens, and in this way obey the law of Christ.
GALATIANS 6:2 NLT

Love and sacrifice is the law of Christ. "Bear ye one another's burdens, and so fulfill the law of Christ." The law of Christ is the bearing of others' burdens, the sharing of others' griefs, sacrificing yourself for another. —A.B. Simpson, The Self Life and the Christ Life

When we share the weight of our loads with others, it becomes lighter to carry. We experience this as we offer our worries to the Lord, but we also find it true in the tangible support of community. We weren't created to rely on ourselves. We weren't made to struggle alone. God put us in his family, and he created us for community.

Community care is one of the most beautiful expressions of God's love in practice. We are all human and struggle, and it is a powerful thing to lean on each other through these times. It can be difficult to admit our need. But it is a strength to admit weakness to one another and share the burdens in order to fulfill the law of Christ. It is the way he wants us to live.

Pray for courage and willingness to share burdens with others.

BEAUTIFUL IN TIME

He has made everything beautiful in its time. Also He has put eternity in their hearts, except that no one can find out the work that God does from beginning to end.

Ecclesiastes 3:11 NKJV

God never hurries. There are no deadlines against which He must work. Only to know this is to quiet our spirits and relax our nerves.
—A.W. Tozer, The Pursuit of God

We are all at different stages of becoming. We are blooming into life, though some of us may need more nurture and attention at the stage we're in. We can trust God as the most skilled gardener to prune and tend to us.

Everything is made beautiful in its time. If we're waiting on our moment of breakthrough, let's not lose hope. Comparison will keep us from contentedness with the gifts of the present. In every stage, there are gifts. Flowers bloom for a little while, but the work that goes on under the surface before and after is just as important. Trust that God knows what he's doing at each step, and it is all for your good.

Ask for perspective to see what season you're in and what God is doing.

COMMIT TO GOD

Commit to the Lord whatever you do,
and he will establish your plans.
Proverbs 16:3 niv

Nothing is well done without prayer for the simple reason that it leaves God out of the account. —E. M. Bounds, The Weapon of Prayer

God loves to bless the work of our hands, especially when we invite him into the process. If we want to walk in the ways of Christ, and to know the power of his breakthrough in our lives, we cannot leave him out of the equation. When we commit what we do to him, doing our best with what we know and have, and follow his lead as we go, we will know the power of his blessing over our work.

We don't have to be in full-time ministry to do this. God is with us in the workplace as much as he is in our places of worship. He is honored by the posture of our hearts and by walking in integrity before him.

Take a moment each day to commit your work to the Lord.

ENCOUNTERING GOD'S LOVE

He gave himself for us to redeem us from all lawlessness and to cleanse for himself a people for his own possession, eager to do good works.

Titus 2:14 CSB

Whether we realize it or not, prayer is the encounter of God's thirst with ours. God thirsts that we may thirst for him.
—St. Augustine, The Eighty-Three Different Questions

Prayer puts us in the path of God's overwhelming love for us. Whatever we bring him, we can be sure the path to his presence is already full of his love, his thirst, drawing us to himself. Our hunger for him? It is a small reflection of the hunger he has for us to know him. All that we experience in passionate pursuit of God originated in his heart. To know him is to love him, and to love him is to know that we were created in his image.

Those who hunger and thirst for righteousness will be filled. The beautiful mystery behind this is that the hunger and thirst we feel for God is nothing compared to his hunger and thirst for us. There is so much more passion in his heart than we can comprehend.

Ask the Lord to reveal the power of his love for you.

INNER STRENGTH

I ask the Father in his great glory to give you the power to be strong inwardly through his Spirit.
EPHESIANS 3:16 NCV

The primary business I must attend to every day is to fellowship with the Lord. The first concern is not how much I might serve the Lord, but how my inner man might be nourished.
—George Müller, Narratives

If we want to be strong in mind, spirit, and heart, we cannot neglect time spent with the Lord in fellowship. As we pray, direct our hearts to the Lord in worship, and read his Word, our inner world is strengthened by his Spirit.

Every day is a new opportunity to strengthen our hearts in him. It doesn't matter what we did or didn't do yesterday. Today is the day we have. This is the moment we can choose what we will do. What does your inner world need to be nourished? Where do you need strength? Where do you need wisdom? Where do you need direction? Bring yourself to the throne of grace even now in prayer.

Spirit strength is available today. Pray for the Lord to meet you in your weakness.

OBEDIENCE IS HONORABLE

Behold, to obey is better than sacrifice,
and to listen than the fat of rams.
1 SAMUEL 15:22 ESV

The one who expects God to do as he asks Him must on his part do whatever God bids him.
—R. A. Torrey, How to Pray

God's ways are not thrown together on a whim. He doesn't lead us just to abandon us, and he doesn't ask us to do something that leads us to harm. God knows better than we do. Do we trust him enough to follow his example? Do we trust him to help us as we obey his Word?

Relationship with God isn't one-sided. It's not all about what we do, and it's not all about what God does. It is reciprocal, or at least it's meant to be. If we have great expectations of God and yet never follow-through with what he's given us to do, we don't have much to stand on. God helps those who call out to him.

Is there something you're resisting following through on? Ask the Lord for strength, and step out in faith.

BOWLS OF INCENSE

When He had taken the scroll, the four living creatures and the twenty-four elders fell down before the Lamb, each one holding a harp and golden bowls full of incense, which are the prayers of the saints.
Revelation 5:8 nasb

The men of mighty prayer are men of spiritual might. Prayers never die.
—E. M. Bounds, Power Through Prayer

The prayers of God's people don't disintegrate or degrade. They don't die. They are before the Lord. The book of Revelation describes the prayers of the saints (God's people) as being in golden bowls of incense. The fragrance of your prayer lingers in the presence of the Lord.

Prayer is a powerful way to connect to God, but it's also a privilege to partner your prayer with those of others. The Lord can recognize the fragrance of the prayers of his people, and he will follow through in faithful love in response. When your timing passes, his has not. Don't be discouraged. Remember God will continue to do all that he has promised, and part of his promise is that he will never leave or forsake you.

Offer your prayers as incense, a fragrant offering to the Lord.

FIRST STEPS

It is impossible to please God without faith. Anyone who wants to come to him must believe that God exists and that he rewards those who sincerely seek him.

Hebrews 11:6 NLT

Understanding is the reward of faith. Therefore, seek not to understand that you may believe, but believe that you may understand.
—St. Augustine, Tractates on the Gospel of John

We don't need to wait to feel the assurance of faith before we come to the Lord in prayer. If we have any inclination to pray, that is a seed of faith in us. God welcomes us, and he gives understanding in response.

You don't need the answers in order to pray. In fact, faith doesn't require answers to move. You have questions? Bring them to God! Don't hold back your curiosity from the one who made you. He isn't threatened by your questions; he knows them all before you ask him. He delights to meet you in the space between question and answer, and he will show you what you could not know without his perspective. Trust him to meet you.

Do you have questions? Bring them to God. He doesn't need false confidence. He wants what is on your heart.

FOUNDATIONS

"If My people who are called by My name will humble themselves, and pray and seek My face, and turn from their wicked ways, then I will hear from heaven, and will forgive their sin and heal their land."
2 CHRONICLES 7:14 NKJV

The great cry of our day is work, new organizations, new methods, and new machinery. The great need of our day is prayer.
—R. A. Torrey, How to Pray

When we are too quick to move to solutions rather than praying for wisdom, discernment, and clarity, we miss out on a powerful opportunity. God's Spirit knows better than we do what is needed. While we might be itching to act, the wise thing is to take a step back and prayerfully consider first.

Fear is hasty, but peace takes the proper time. If you feel rushed to move ahead, but you don't feel clear on what it is your moving toward, take a step back. Pray. God meets the humble and brings healing when they pray, seek his face, and turn from sin. Do that today, and you will know the power of his wisdom as it guides you.

Instead of rushing to move ahead, take time to humble yourself, pray, and ask for the Lord's guidance.

FULL PORTION

I say to myself, "The LORD is my portion;
therefore I will wait for him."
LAMENTATIONS 3:24 NIV

An infinite God can give all of Himself to each of His children. He does not distribute Himself that each may have a part, but to each one He gives all of Himself as fully as if there were no others.
—A. W. Tozer, The Pursuit of God

If you care at all about fairness, you might wonder whether some people get more of God while others get less. The truth is that the Lord gives the same portion to all who yield their lives to him—the fullness of who he is. We might have differing levels of understanding or experience, but our access to God is the same.

If you are in Christ, you are completely new. You are pure in the forgiveness of his love. You are filled with grace, mercy, and peace. There is nothing that God withholds from those who walk in the light of his love. Nothing!

Have you been living like you a full or partial portion of the Lord? Ask for greater revelation of his fullness today.

HE STRAIGHTENS THE PATH

In all your ways know him,
and he will make your paths straight.
Proverbs 3:6 CSB

Our prayers need to be focused upon the present. We must trust God today, and leave the morrow entirely with Him. The present is ours; the future belongs to God. Prayer is the task and duty of each recurring day -- daily prayer for daily needs.
—E. M. Bounds, The Necessity of Prayer

When we acknowledge the Lord in our lives, committing each day to him, he leads us in his grace and straightens the path. We don't have to wait to walk until the path is clear. We can trust his guiding hand as he leads us step by step.

Instead of praying for the future, focus your prayers on today. What do you need today? Do you already know the step that is yours to take? One step at a time; that is how we get anywhere, including how we get to God's eternal kingdom. Let your daily prayers reflect your daily needs, and trust God with tomorrow. He will straighten the path as you go.

What are today's needs? Pray for them.

ABUNDANT READINESS

"If you abide in me, and my words abide in you, ask whatever you wish, and it will be done for you."
John 15:7 ESV

Every child of God is not called by the Lord to establish schools and orphan houses and to trust in the Lord for means for them. Yet, there is no reason why you may not experience, far more abundantly than we do now, His willingness to answer the prayers of His children.
—George Müller, Narratives

No matter what it is you do, you can know the all-surpassing goodness of God in response to your prayers. You don't have to travel the world, giving your life to the poor to know God's presence or favor. Submit your life to God—as it is—and he will lead you into his fullness.

As we abide in Christ, we get to know what he is like. We come to understand what his love looks like and requires. Our prayers become reflections of his character and of God's desire to meet his people with kindness and healing. Get to know Christ more, through the Word and through prayer, and your prayer life will become a garden where the fruit of God's Spirit grows.

What prayer is on your heart to ask the Lord today?

COMPLETELY KNOWN

Our high priest is able to understand our weaknesses. He was tempted in every way that we are, but he did not sin.

HEBREWS 4:15 NCV

Sometimes, when your child talks, your friends cannot understand what he says; but the mother understands very well. So if our prayer comes right from the heart, God understands our language.
—D. L. Moody, Prevailing Prayer

Isn't it wonderful to know you don't have to explain yourself to God? He knows you through and through, and his love for you is deeper than the love of a mother. He understands you perfectly, and he knows how to translate your jumbled thoughts. What you don't even know to put into words? He knows. What you're just discovering about yourself? He's been patiently waiting for you to get to this place. He isn't surprised by a thing about you.

Don't let the judgments of others cloud what God thinks of you. Ask for his pure perspective. He doesn't shame you for your weaknesses, and he won't humiliate you. His love strengthens your identity, and his grace empowers you to live with integrity.

Thank God for how wonderfully he loves you, and let his love be what fuels your confidence and identity.

HIGH AND EXALTED

I saw the Lord sitting on a throne, lofty and exalted, with the train of His robe filling the temple.

Isaiah 6:1 NASB

In prayer we stand where angels bow with veiled faces; there, even there, the cherubim and seraphim adore, before that selfsame throne to which our prayers ascend. —C. H. Spurgeon, The Throne of Grace

Our prayers bring us to the throne of grace where God is enrobed in majesty. Isaiah said he saw the Lord sitting on a throne and the train of his robe filled the whole temple. Can you imagine the grandeur he witnessed? God is close to us, but he is also incomparably powerful, glorious, and worthy of our praise.

May your prayers not stay relegated to the realm of needs today. Take time to worship and honor the worthy one. He is high and lifted up, and he welcomes you into his presence. Ask the Holy Spirit to give you a glimpse into the holy of holies, where he dwells. One glimpse can make everything else fade away.

Worship the Lord for who he is, and ask for eyes to see and a heart to comprehend what he is truly like.

FREEDOM FOR YOUR SOUL

He has removed our sins as far from us
as the east is from the west.
PSALM 103:12 NLT

Sometimes I go to God and say, "God, if Thou dost never answer another prayer while I live on this earth, I will still worship Thee as long as I live and in the ages to come for what Thou hast done already." God's already put me so far in debt that if I were to live one million millenniums I couldn't pay Him for what He's done for me.
—A.W. Tozer, Worship: The Missing Jewel

We could never repay the enormous debt Christ paid for us on the Cross. He is our salvation: setting our souls free, giving us a new identity in him, and removing the guilt of our sins. He will never hold against us what he has already forgiven. Isn't that good news?

God's grace is generous. It can't run dry. Let's never keep ourselves from the forgiveness that he so freely offers us. There is liberty in his love and merciful peace in his presence. Why would we keep ourselves locked in cages of shame, fear, or cycles of sin when he holds the key to our freedom?

Worship the Lord for the freedom he gives you; there is greater liberty for you today. Simply ask, receive, and walk in it.

CHILDLIKE FAITH

Jesus said, "Let the little children come to Me, and do not forbid them; for of such is the kingdom of heaven."
Matthew 19:14 NKJV

God's revelation does not need the light of human genius, the polish and strength of human culture, the brilliancy of human thought, the force of human brains to adorn or enforce it; but it does demand the simplicity, the docility, humility, and faith of a child's heart.
—E. M. Bounds, Power Through Prayer

Children rely on the leadership of their parents. They are dependent on their care. God is the perfect parent—the good Father. He never withholds what his children need. We don't have to pretend to know what we can't. We trust him to guide, teach, and correct us, and he does so in kindness.

Let childlike faith lead you in prayer. Humble your heart before the Lord and remember that he is God, and he knows better than you what is needed today. He wants you to delight in the gifts he offers and trust him. Can you do that?

Come to the Lord in simple, childlike faith today.

PATIENCE IN HIS PRESENCE

Being strengthened with all power according to his glorious might so that you may have great endurance and patience.
COLOSSIANS 1:11 NIV

Too often we knock at mercy's door, and then run away, instead of waiting for an entrance and an answer. —D. L. Moody, Prevailing Prayer

Prayer is an invitation. It is a doorway to the presence of God. When we come to the Lord in prayer, let's not be so quick to move on. As we wait on his presence, listening for his voice, his peace will wash over us.

God does not withhold from those who earnestly seek him. When we press in, in the place of prayer, we don't just talk the whole time. We offer our heartfelt prayer, and then we take time to wait and see if God has anything to reveal to us through his Spirit or his Word. The more we listen for his whisper, the more attuned we become to his voice, recognizing when he speaks.

Spend time waiting in God's presence after you offer God the prayers of your heart.

MODELED AFTER JESUS

Do nothing from selfish ambition or conceit, but in humility count others more significant than yourselves.

PHILIPPIANS 2:3 ESV

Meekness and lowliness of heart are to be the distinguishing feature of the disciple, just as they were of the Master. And further, that this humility is not something that will come of itself, but that it must be made the object of special desire, prayer, faith, and practice.
—Andrew Murray, Humility: The Beauty of Holiness

Jesus, the Master, set the example for his disciples: both those who followed him in his ministry, and those of us who have committed our lives to him since. The ways of Jesus are the ways of the disciple. This includes cultivating and maintaining a humble heart.

We will not one day wake up magically humbled and ready to serve. It is in practice—in prayer, faith, and action—that we transform our hearts and minds in the love of Christ. It is our daily work to actively humble ourselves before the Lord and others, and choose the path of love in our interactions.

Pray for a heart that is willing to serve others, and put your faith into practice today.

JOYFUL GRATITUDE

A desire accomplished is sweet to the soul,
But it is an abomination to fools to depart from evil.
Proverbs 13:19 NKJV

The joy which answers to prayer give, cannot be described; and the impetus which they afford to the spiritual life is exceedingly great.
—George Müller, Answers to Prayer

The practice of remembering the promises that God has fulfilled is one that cultivates gratitude and connects with joy. It is easy to move from the place of relief to the next thing, but we miss out when we don't take the time to properly honor the fulfillment of our once-held longings.

Take a look at your life. What old dreams are you now living in? Which longings did you have that are now fulfilled? Instead of taking your present life for granted, take time to thank God for the goodness he has shown you in practical ways. What he has done, he will continue to do. Cultivate a heart of gratitude in prayer before him today.

Thank God for each blessing that was once a prayer. His faithfulness is worth noting!

Sweet Surrender

Guide me in your truth and teach me,
for you are the God of my salvation;
I wait for you all day long.
Psalm 25:5 csb

I am no longer my own, but Yours. Put me to what You will, rank me with whom You will; put me to doing, put me to suffering; let me be employed for You or laid aside for You, exalted for You or brought low for You; let me be full, let me be empty; let me have all things, let me have nothing; I freely and wholeheartedly yield all things to Your pleasure and disposal. —John Wesley, Covenant Prayer

It is a beautiful freedom to get to the place of surrender before the Lord. No matter the circumstances we face, nor the challenges that arise, we have a faithfully good shepherd. He knows what he is doing in and around us, and we can trust him to take care of us.

You cannot control tomorrow, but you can know the power of God's peace today. You can work, walk, and serve in loving trust as you yield your heart to him. He is faithful, and he will not let you down.

Pray Wesley's prayer today, or adapt it to make it your own.

DON'T HOLD BACK

"Take My yoke upon you and learn from Me, for I am gentle and humble in heart, and you will find rest for your souls. For My yoke is comfortable, and My burden is light."
MATTHEW 11:29-30 NASB

Let your cares drive you to God. I shall not mind if you have many of them if each one leads you to prayer. If every fret makes you lean more on the Beloved, it will be a benefit.
—C. H. Spurgeon, A Cure for Care

You cannot weary God with what's on your mind or heart. You can't exhaust his patient love. Jesus invites you to bring him your worries, your cares, and your questions. He welcomes all of you. But this is not where the journey ends. He offers you his partnership, and he does all the heavy lifting.

Take his yoke upon you, and you will find rest for your soul. Learn from him, and you will be delighted with the powerful wisdom rooted in peace, love, hope, and joy that you find. His yoke is easy, and his burden is light.

Bring every care to the Lord in prayer, and receive what he offers in return.

RICH SUBSTANCE

Let the message about Christ, in all its richness, fill your lives. Teach and counsel each other with all the wisdom he gives. Sing psalms and hymns and spiritual songs to God with thankful hearts.

COLOSSIANS 3:16 NLT

Prayer that is born of meditation upon the Word of God is the prayer that soars upward most easily to God's listening ears.
—R. A. Torrey, How to Pray

The message of Christ is full of substance that is richly wise, beautiful, refreshing, and deeply satisfying. When we meditate on the Word, our hearts and minds align with the Spirit of God, and he answers our questions in that place. There is a strong foundation of faith in the Word to stand upon. Let us begin our prayers from that place today.

Perhaps there is a powerful Scripture that you keep coming back to. Maybe you have been pondering the meaning of a specific passage. As you meditate on the Word, bringing your thoughtful attention to God's revelation of wisdom, invite the Spirit to meet you in that place. Let your prayers flow naturally from what comes up. God not only listens, but he also answers.

Pick a passage of Scripture to meditate on and pray from today.

WORSHIP THE LORD

Rest in the LORD, and wait patiently for Him;
Do not fret because of him who prospers in his way.
PSALM 37:7 NKJV

Each time, before you intercede, be quiet first, and worship God in His glory. Think of what He can do, and how He delights to hear the prayers of His redeemed people. Think of your place and privilege in Christ, and expect great things!
—Andrew Murray, With Christ in the School of Prayer

Beginning our prayer time with worship sets our hearts in the right perspective. When we remember who God is, we can prayerfully bring everything else before him without having to beg. He is Almighty God, and all things are possible through him.

Our expectation in prayer grows as we come to understand the power of Christ. The more we worship him in spirit and in truth, the more our hearts grow in hopeful expectation. We have tasted and seen the goodness of the Lord. And there is more to feast upon in the presence of his faithful love.

Spend time in adoration of Christ before you move into petitioning him in prayer.

GOD IS NEAR

God did this so that they would seek him and perhaps reach out for him and find him, though he is not far from any one of us.
ACTS 17:27 NIV

We need never shout across the spaces to an absent God. He is nearer than our own soul, closer than our most secret thoughts.
—A. W. Tozer, The Pursuit of God

God is not far away from you. Right here, right now, where you sit in this moment, he is with you. He is nearer than your own soul. He is closer than the air in your lungs.

What if your prayer were less of a reach to the heavens today and more of a turning of your attention to the presence of God where you are? In Psalm 139, the psalmist declares that there is nowhere you can flee the presence of God. If you were to go to the highest heights or the deepest depths, God would be right there with you. Let his presence be your comfort and your confidence. He is near!

Whisper your prayer to God as an act of faith that he is present, listening, and attentive.

FOR ALL PEOPLE

First of all, then, I urge that supplications, prayers, intercessions, and thanksgivings be made for all people.
1 Timothy 2:1 ESV

Pray for "all men." We usually pray more for things than we do for men. Our prayers should be thrown across their pathway as they rush in their downward course to a lost eternity.
—E. M. Bounds, Power Through Prayer

Focusing our prayers on people rather than things can redirect our hearts in love. When we only think about stuff, we disconnect our need from community. People are what God cares about first and foremost. Do our prayers reflect that?

Today is a perfect opportunity to refocus our prayers. When we would rather pray for situations than people, we have some aligning to do. God loves to heal, to restore, and to redeem, but it is always based in his love of his creation (you and me). Jesus instructed us to not only pray for those we like, but to also pray for enemies. Let us bring those we struggle with before the throne of grace and pray for God's powerful love to move in our hearts and in their lives.

Spend time praying for someone you don't like.

SECURELY ATTACHED

May the Lord lead your hearts into God's love and Christ's patience.
2 THESSALONIANS 3:5 NCV

Many times I am forced in my prayers, first to beg of God that he would take mine heart, and set it on himself in Christ, and when it is there, that he would keep it there.
—John Bunyan, A Discourse Touching Prayer

God's love is the foundation of everything. It is who he is. First John 4 sets us straight on this matter. "Love comes from God. Everyone who loves has become God's child and knows God… because God is love" (verses 7-8). God's love is the basis of all he does, all he is, and all we should ever endeavor to be.

Love is patient. It is kind. It does not boast. It is not easily offended. It is gracious, full of peace, and powerfully secure. Let us ground ourselves in God's love, remembering there is no limit to his mercy, and let our prayers flow from that place. God is not bothered when we reach out to him. He delights in it.

Focus on the powerful love of God as you pray today.

Daily Business

That your faith might not be based on human wisdom
but on God's power.
1 Corinthians 2:5 csb

Prayer must not be our chance work, but our daily business, our habit and vocation. —C. H. Spurgeon, Evening by Evening

What a business to make of ourselves every day—to pray! It does not cost us a thing or require acquiring anything we don't already have. We have access to the King of kings through Jesus Christ. Why wouldn't we make prayer a daily practice, when it offers us so much? There is fellowship, power, and love. There is peace, joy, and hope in connecting to our Provider. There is all we need, and so much more that we can't imagine, in the presence of God.

If we want our faith to be based on God's power, we have to know what to expect. We have to know the one who holds and wields that power. Let's make it our daily business to pray, not only to receive, but to know the one who formed us, called us, and equips us as his own.

Schedule prayer at least once a day, and do it faithfully. (Try pairing it with something you already do—like washing the dishes, driving to work, or brushing your teeth)

PRACTICE OF CULTIVATION

Then the Lord God took the man and put him in the Garden of Eden to cultivate it and tend it.

Genesis 2:15 nasb

Prayer not only teaches and strengthens one for work, work teaches and strengthens one for prayer.
—Andrew Murray, With Christ in the School of Prayer

Much of life is not one-sided. Think about it this way. When farmers tend the soil, plant the seeds, and pick the harvest, do they do it just to keep their hands busy? No, their tending to the earth and planting seeds reaps a harvest that they can eat, sell, and provide for their community. The farmer readies the land, and the land's response strengthens the farmer.

When we pray, we are not only praying for the strength to do what we are called to do. As we walk out our calling, doing the daily work that is ours to do, our prayers are also fed and our focus sharpened. Let's not relegate prayer to the quiet moments, but let's see the cycle of our living as feeding into it.

Let your work be an offering to God even as your prayers are.

INFINITE RESOURCES

Yours, O Lord, is the greatness, the power, the glory, the victory, and the majesty. Everything in the heavens and on earth is yours, O Lord, and this is your kingdom. We adore you as the one who is over all things.

1 Chronicles 29:11 NLT

Few Christians have anything but a vague idea of the power of prayer; fewer still have any experience of that power. The Church seems almost wholly unaware of the power God puts into her hand; this spiritual carte blanche on the infinite resources of God's wisdom and power is rarely, if ever, used—never used to the full measure of honouring God. —E. M. Bounds, Purpose in Prayer

God is not strapped for resources. He has everything we need, and he is more than willing to give us what we request. He takes care of us physically, spiritually, emotionally, and socially. There isn't an area of our lives untouched by his gracious generosity.

Why, oh why, then, would we not press in to know the power of God's limitless mercy, grace, justice, and peace in greater measure? Our faith rests on God's faithfulness, not on our abilities. Our soul's hunger is fed by God's nourishment, not by what we scrape and scrimp for. He is more than willing to lavish his powerful resources in and through us.

Let your prayers match the wealth of God's power.

A PRIORITY

When He had sent the multitudes away, He went up on the mountain by Himself to pray. Now when evening came, He was alone there.

MATTHEW 14:23 NKJV

The man who would truly know God must give time to Him.
—A. W. Tozer, The Pursuit of God

Jesus made spending time alone with his heavenly Father a priority. He knew he needed that time to be refreshed in his presence, and so do we. When we refuse to give time and attention to God, we miss out on the power of his wisdom, leadership, and ministering comfort. Everything that we need is found in him. Why would we waste time on things that distract us rather than connect us to our life-giving source?

There are responsibilities we can't get out of. There is work to be done. But we don't have to trudge through these and let others dictate what we do in our personal time. What a wonderful oasis of peace we will find if we choose to go to God in prayer often.

How much time do you give to God each day?

IN THE STILLNESS

Be still before the Lord, all mankind, because he has roused himself from his holy dwelling.
Zechariah 2:13 NIV

When we first come into God's presence, we should be silent before Him.
—R. A. Torrey, How to Pray

What a powerful practice it is to quiet ourselves before the Lord before we say a thing. When we give the Lord our time and attention, there's no rush to move from stillness to activity. We need room to adore, to meditate, and to consider thoughtfully the power of God. We need space to reside in his presence.

Are your prayer times rushed, or do you take the time to sit quietly in God's presence on a regular basis? Haste is a sign of desperation, but it can also be a condition of avoidance. When we learn to press into prayerful meditation with an open heart before God, we allow God to meet us and fill the spaces that need his care.

How often do you sit in stillness before God?

DELIGHTED IN

The LORD your God is in your midst,
a mighty one who will save;
he will rejoice over you with gladness;
he will quiet you by his love;
he will exult over you with loud singing.
ZEPHANIAH 3:17 ESV

See, loving heart, how He delights in you. When you lean your head on His bosom, you not only receive, but you give Him joy; when you gaze with love upon His all-glorious face, you not only obtain comfort, but impart delight. —C. H. Spurgeon, Evening by Evening

God is delighted in you, rejoicing with gladness. He has nothing but love for you. Those weaknesses you see so clearly in yourself? They don't distract God from his mercy. He loves you fully. When you learn to accept the power of his kindness, his delight in you becomes the fuel for your delight in him. And on it goes.

You are you because of who God made you. Your quirks bring him delight. Self-hatred is not a fruit of the Spirit! He longs for you to live in the light of his love, free to be who he created you to be.

Ask the Lord to reveal the power of his delight over you today.

GOOD GIFTS

"If you sinful people know how to give good gifts to your children, how much more will your heavenly Father give good gifts to those who ask him."

Matthew 7:11 NLT

Answered prayer is the interchange of love between the Father and His child. —Andrew Murray, With Christ in the School of Prayer

The Father delights in giving good gifts to his children. Even human parents know how to provide for their children in love. That reflects a small percentage of God's kindness. His love is pure, and he offers it freely. He is the perfect parent to all who come to him through his Son.

Do you pray expecting the bare minimum? Do you hesitate to ask for what you need or want? God's love is a foundation of secure faithfulness. You don't have to worry about what he thinks of you. He knows you best, and he loves you most. He won't misunderstand you or turn your prayers into a way to shame, control, or hold you hostage. His love liberates. Do you know the love of your perfect Father?

Ask God for greater revelation of his goodness as your Father.

PRAYERS AND PROMISES

These all died in faith, not having received the things promised, but having seen them and greeted them from afar, and having acknowledged that they were strangers and exiles on the earth.
Hebrews 11:13 ESV

Prayers are deathless. They outlive the lives of those who uttered them.
—E. M. Bounds, Purpose in Prayer

Though Abraham did not receive the fullness of God's promise in his lifetime, does that mean God's promise was null? No! He continued, and still continues, to faithfully fulfill his promise. In the same way, our prayers don't end with our breath. They don't have a time limit. Our faith is based on God's faithfulness, not on the timelines of this earth.

Prayer is never wasted effort. The prayers of the righteous are powerful. We see in part now, and we know in part, but one day everything will be as clear as the sunniest day. Understanding will be deep and grounded. Until that day, let's rejoice in the glimpses we get, for we do get many. Let's open our eyes to the fingerprints of God's mercy around us, and thank him for what he continually works out in faithful love.

Ask for eyes to see where the thread of God's faithfulness weaves through your life.

SUFFICIENT GRACE

"My grace is sufficient for you, for power is perfected in weakness." Most gladly, therefore, I will rather boast about my weaknesses, so that the power of Christ may dwell in me.
2 Corinthians 12:9 NASB

One morning as I was again at prayer, and trembling under the fear of this, That no word of God could help me, that piece of a sentence darted in upon me, My grace is sufficient.
—John Bunyan, Grace Abounding to the Chief of Sinners

There is no amount of weakness that God's grace cannot strengthen. When we don't have much to give, the answer isn't to try harder. It's to pray and ask the Lord for his strength. It's to lean on the presence of God, and to trust that he can do much more with our weakness than we can do on our strongest day.

Power is perfected in weakness. Don't despise the things that make you feel the extent of your humanity. Lean into the love of your Father, and let his generous grace meet you there. When you are vulnerable, God's love is powerful.

Thank God for the weaknesses you struggle to accept, and invite his grace to move in you.

UNSEEN POWER

Faith shows the reality of what we hope for; it is the evidence of things we cannot see.
HEBREWS 11:1 NLT

Faith does not operate in the realm of the possible. There is no glory for God in that which is humanly possible. Faith begins where man's power ends. —George Müller, Narratives

We often limit our prayers to what we know, but God is able to do far more than we could ever think to ask him! When we stretch our imagination to ask God for what is possible with him, and not what we are used to, we invite the strengthening and stretching of our faith to meet his faithfulness.

God is gracious. He knows we cannot see the full picture. He realizes that we are prone to get comfortable in the environments we are used to. Don't let your experience dictate what you ask of God. Let God's Word, his powerful ability, and his love draw you into greater expectation of his goodness!

Ask for what you are really hoping for!

PAIRING OUR PRAYERS

Through Jesus let us always offer to God our sacrifice of praise, coming from lips that speak his name.
HEBREWS 13:15 NCV

It is prayer and earnestness; prayer and watchfulness; prayer and thanksgiving. It is an instructive fact that throughout Scripture prayer is always linked with something else. —D. L. Moody, Prevailing Prayer

Prayer is a simple act, but it is not something that has to look the same each time we do it. Prayer, when paired with another activity or posture of the heart, moves us further into relating to God.

Prayer doesn't only need to happen when we feel like it. It is in those times when we struggle to even want to reach out to the Lord that we can offer him the sacrifice of our praise. When we train our hearts to turn to him, no matter the day, the hour, the circumstance, or the struggle, we train our hearts to connect to him.

Pair your prayer with something you do today.

DEEP CALLS TO DEEP

Deep calls unto deep at the noise of Your waterfalls;
All Your waves and billows have gone over me.
PSALM 42:7 NKJV

The yearning to know what cannot be known, to comprehend the incomprehensible, to touch and taste the unapproachable, arises from the image of God in the nature of man. Deep calleth unto deep, and though polluted and landlocked by the mighty disaster theologians call the Fall, the soul senses its origin and longs to return to its source.
—A.W. Tozer, The Pursuit of God

Our souls long for the Lord for the things we have not known. We long for connection. In prayer, the depth of our need meets the depth of God's love. There is more longing in his heart than we can imagine. There is more grace in his nature than we can receive. There is more power in his presence than we could ever experience.

Let the depth of your need and longing lead you to the depth of God's goodness today.

Ask God to overflow your deep need with his generous goodness.

JOYFUL SATISFACTION

May the God of hope fill you with all joy and peace as you trust in him, so that you may overflow with hope by the power of the Holy Spirit.
ROMANS 15:13 NIV

The reality is that a heart desire for prayer is lacking. Many do not know how to spend half an hour with God! It is not that they absolutely do not pray; they may pray every day—but they have no joy in prayer. Joy is the sign that God is everything to you.
—Andrew Murray, The Prayer Life

As we trust the Lord, he fills us with the fruit of his presence. That is, we receive the fullness of his Spirit in the evidence of: love, joy, peace, patience, kindness, goodness, faithfulness, gentleness, and self-control (Galatians 5:22-23). In knowing God, we experience his peace and the joy of his fellowship.

Are you lacking in joy? Don't punish yourself. Spend time in prayer and ask the Lord to meet you in that place. Ask him to fill you with his presence so joy bubbles up from the inside of your soul. Look to the light of his face, and your own will shine.

Rejoice in the Lord today, and thank him for his power as you pray.

HEALING POWER

He was pierced for our transgressions;
he was crushed for our iniquities;
upon him was the chastisement that brought us peace,
and with his wounds we are healed.
ISAIAH 53:5 ESV

The streaming wounds of Jesus are the sure guarantees for answered prayer. —C. H. Spurgeon, The Golden Key of Prayer

In Christ, we have the fulfillment of every promise of God. He is the embodiment of the Father's faithful love. When he died on the cross and rose again three days later, the power of death was overcome. We are not living under a curse if we are in the light of Christ. We are free, we are connected to the Creator, and we are healed.

Every promise finds its fullness in Christ. Every answered prayer is found in his fellowship. Let's not neglect praising and thanking him for his sacrifice. He broke the chains, lifted our shame, and opened the door for our liberty. Praise Jesus!

Thank the Lord for his sacrifice and what it means for you.

SEEK FIRST

"Seek first the kingdom of God and his righteousness, and all these things will be provided for you."
Matthew 6:33 CSB

The sooner I learn to forget myself in the desire that He may be glorified, the richer will be the blessing that prayer will bring to myself. No one ever loses by what he sacrifices to the Father.
—Andrew Murray, With Christ in the School of Prayer

The first step of knowing what God requires of us is to know him. We know him by seeking him. We seek his kingdom by following the law of love that Christ exemplified in his life. When God's opinion becomes most important, we let go of what others may think. Every sacrifice becomes worth it.

In prayer, seek God first. Seek his righteousness. You can be sure that God will provide everything you need as you walk in his ways. There isn't anything he withholds from those who love him. The provision comes as you walk the path he's laid for you.

Seek first God's kingdom in all you do today, including in prayer.

UNSEEN TREASURES

"When you pray, don't be like the hypocrites. They love to stand in the synagogues and on the street corners and pray so people will see them. I tell you the truth, they already have their full reward."

MATTHEW 6:5 NCV

Public prayers of are of little value unless they are founded on or followed up by private praying. —E. M. Bounds, Power Through Prayer

If our prayers are based on how impressive they seem to others, their power ends right there. Our public prayers should reflect our private prayers. We don't have to pray with beautiful language or for minutes on end. Our prayers should come from the pure place of our hearts. God already knows what's in us anyway.

It is much more important how we pray when we're alone. A life of confidence in the Lord is cultivated in the quiet place, in the moments of surrender that no one else witnesses. The aim of our prayer life shouldn't be to impress others but to reflect the relationship we have with the Lord.

God becomes your confidence as you pursue him. Let your prayers reflect that pursuit.

VESSELS OF HIS GLORY

We have this treasure in earthen containers, so that the extraordinary greatness of the power will be of God and not from ourselves.
2 CORINTHIANS 4:7 NASB

I have now concentrated all my prayers into one, and that one prayer is this, that I may die to self, and live wholly to Him.
—C. H. Spurgeon, The Saint and His Saviour

When we surrender our lives fully to the Lord, his life in us becomes our strength. We no longer rely on our own abilities to get us through. We get to partner with what God has put in us and follow his lead. The power of God is put on display in those who trust him to do what they cannot.

If the only prayer you were to pray would be to die to yourself (everything that stands against Christ and the law of his love) and live wholly for the Lord, it would encompass most everything you need to live a life empowered by his Spirit.

Your body is weak, but God's power is strong. Pray and ask that he would be glorified in your life.

BACK TO THE START

"The seed on the rocky soil represents those who hear the message and immediately receive it with joy. But since they don't have deep roots, they don't last long. They fall away as soon as they have problems or are persecuted for believing God's word."

Matthew 13:20-21 NLT

The man that takes up religion for the world will throw away religion for the world. —John Bunyan, The Pilgrim's Progress

If our faith is based on what others think of us, we may grow some at first, but we will quickly wither when that faith is tested. God honors the hunger of those who look for him and depend on him. If you find yourself wondering what the foundation of your faith is, ask the Lord to bring you back to the start. Ask him to strengthen you in the living expression of his love as it transforms your mind, heart, and life.

You cannot care more about what others think than you do of what God thinks of you. To say it another way, your life reflects your values. If they are shallow, the fruit of your life will be, too. If you want a deep faith, pray that God's values become as dear to you as your own.

Ask the Lord to bring you back to his love as the foundation of your faith.

SPIRITUAL OXYGEN

I will sing to the Lord as long as I live;
I will sing praise to my God while I have my being.
Psalm 104:33 NKJV

Man can as well live physically without breathing, as spiritually without praying. —D. L. Moody, Prevailing Prayer

No one can survive without breathing. It is an element of living. In the same way, our spirits need connection to God. Prayer is a basic function of faith. Though we take it for granted, it is key—not only to our survival—but to thriving in Christ.

The quality of the air around us can affect our health. This is true of what we take in spiritually. The Holy Spirit is clarifying for our souls. Fellowship with our Creator is a powerful connection for abundance of all that the Spirit offers—love, joy, peace, patience, kindness—the fullness of his fruit. Not every breath needs to be a deep one, but as we turn our attention to the air entering our lungs, our minds, hearts, and bodies settle in greater calm.

Take a deep spiritual breath in prayer today.

SPIRIT WORK

He who searches our hearts knows the mind of the Spirit, because the Spirit intercedes for God's people in accordance with the will of God.

Romans 8:27 niv

A shaking hand may as well write a line steadily, as we can keep our hearts fixed in prayer without the Spirit of God.
—Thomas Watson, The Ten Commandments

If you're feeling discouraged about your prayer life, take heart. There is one who helps you pray when you don't know what to pray. The Holy Spirit intercedes on our behalf when we don't have the words, and his work in our yielded hearts keeps us before the Father.

The Spirit always prays according to God's will. You can rest in the confidence that what God does, he does exceedingly well. If you are feeling spiritually dry today, invite the Spirit to move in the deep places within you, releasing God's love where deep calls to deep. You don't have to try harder today. Rest and receive, and you will be refreshed in spirit and truth.

Invite the Spirit to read your heart and intercede for you.

Prayerful Action

When he calls to me, I will answer him;
I will be with him in trouble;
I will rescue him and honor him.
Psalm 91:15 esv

This I most firmly believe, that no one ought to expect to see much good resulting from his labors in word and doctrine, if he is not much given to prayer and meditation. —George Müller, The Life of Trust

Relationship with God is a partnership. We receive the glorious grace of salvation, and Christ sets us free to walk in his love. There is power in the prayerful actions of those who rely on the Lord as their strength.

Ask, and it will be given to you. Seek, and you will find. Knock, and the door will be opened to you. Follow the leadership of love's example in Christ. Do as he said and live out his kindness in your daily life. Love your neighbor, pray for your enemy, and walk humbly with your God. Everything that reveals the wisdom of God through your life is a powerful action.

Put prayer behind your actions, and leave room for God to redirect you in your plans.

HAPPY COMMUNION

We are completely free to enter the Most Holy Place without fear because of the blood of Jesus' death. We can enter through a new and living way that Jesus opened for us. It leads through the curtain—Christ's body.

HEBREWS 10:19-20 NCV

To have God thus near is to enter the holy of holies—to breathe the fragrance of the heavenly air, to walk in Eden's delightful gardens. Nothing but prayer can bring God and man into this happy communion.
—E. M. Bounds, Purpose in Prayer

Nothing separates us from the love of God that is in Christ Jesus our Lord. Nothing! We have an open door to connection with God through Christ, and this is true today. Let prayer be the gateway that brings you before the Prince of Peace.

Adam and Eve walked in the Garden of Eden with God. Faithful men and women of God have fellowshipped with him throughout the ages. And today, we have the privilege of also having this kind of happy communion with the Lord. What treasures there are to be found in his fellowship each and every day!

Walk in the garden of God's goodness in prayer today.

Living Sacrifice

In view of the mercies of God, I urge you to present your bodies as a living sacrifice, holy and pleasing to God; this is your true worship.

Romans 12:1 CSB

It is the privilege of every Christian to live so fully in God that he never gets out of the experienced Presence for one moment.... The whole life becomes a prayer... thoughts become mental prayers, deeds become prayers in action and even sleep may be but unconscious prayer. —A.W. Tozer, The Pursuit of God

All of life can be a fragrant prayer that rises to the throne room of heaven. When we become living sacrifices, surrendered to the Lord and his powerful presence in our lives, the natural becomes supernatural by the life of his Spirit working in us.

We don't have to hold back a thing from the Lord. He will never use what we offer him against us. He will not mistreat or trick us. His intentions are pure, and his love is limitless. Each day, there is nourishment for our souls—exactly what we need in every moment.

Offer yourself as a living sacrifice today, letting your heart remain open before the Lord.

A CLEAN HEART

Create in me a clean heart, God,
And renew a steadfast spirit within me.
Psalm 51:10 NASB

Nothing searches and cleanses the heart like true prayer. It teaches one to ask such questions as these: Do I really desire what I pray for? Am I willing to cast out everything to make room for what God is prepared to give me? Is the prayer of my lips really the prayer of my life?
—Andrew Murray, Experiencing the Holy Spirit

We can't purify our own hearts. That's the work of God. But we can present ourselves before him in prayer and ask that he would create a clean heart, softening the harsh edges of bitterness and purifying our intentions. We don't have to self-protect in his presence. He is pure love, and his mercy washes over us, filling us to overflowing and removing the impurities as he goes.

Stand in the light of God's love today. Before you move on with your day, before you do anything else, ask the Lord to fill you with the power of his presence so that everything else falls away.

Ask the Lord to cleanse your heart in his pure affection today.

OVERCOMERS

Every child of God defeats this evil world, and we achieve this victory through our faith.
1 John 5:4 NLT

Prayer brings blessings to the church. The history of the church has always been a history of grave difficulties to overcome.
—R. A. Torrey, How to Pray

When we find ourselves up against the proverbial wall, it is an invitation for us to trust the Lord, press in with prayer, and wait on his leadership. Countless obstacles were overcome by those who came before us. David defeated Goliath, the Israelites escaped their captors, and Hannah's barren womb conceived.

Life is full of obstacles. We can't avoid them. What if, instead of trying to avoid those tensions we rose in faith by reaching out to the Lord for his heavenly solutions? God is good. He shut the mouths of the lions for Daniel, and he stood in the fire with Shadrach, Meshach, and Abednego. God always has a way for breakthrough.

Pray for the courage of an overcomer.

ECHOING GOD'S PROMISE

"O Lord God, You are God, and Your words are true, and You have promised this goodness to Your servant."
2 Samuel 7:28 NKJV

What is prayer but the promise pleaded? A promise is, so to speak, the raw material of prayer. Prayer irrigates the fields of life with the waters which are stored up in the reservoirs of promise. The promise is the power of prayer. We go to God, and we say to him, "Do as thou hast said. O Lord, here is thy word; we beseech thee fulfil it."
—C. H. Spurgeon, According to Promise

We don't have to keep our prayers to the realm of theory. When we have a promise of God to stand upon, let's pray it right back to the Father. God's promises are yes and amen in Christ. They find their fulfillment in him. We do not have to beg, and we don't have to remind him to be faithful. But the reminder serves our hearts well by feeding our faith.

Let your prayers reflect what God has spoken. Let your prayers flood your own memory with the power of God's truth. He won't leave his promises unanswered.

Do you have a promise of God you're waiting on? Pray it today.

WISE LIVING

Be very careful, then, how you live—not as unwise but as wise, making the most of every opportunity, because the days are evil.
Ephesians 5:15-16 NIV

We do not live in tomorrow but in today. We do not seek tomorrow's grace or tomorrow's bread. They thrive best, and get most out of life, who live in the living present. They pray best who pray for today's needs, not for tomorrow's, which may render our prayers unnecessary and redundant by not existing at all!
—E. M. Bounds, The Necessity of Prayer

Wisdom isn't found in what we plan to do. It is in where the rubber meets the road, in the present moment. How we act today reflects what we believe about God. Let's keep our prayers focused on what is at hand, where God is ready to move.

Today is filled with many opportunities to press into the presence of the Lord. Your prayers don't have to be formal or uninterrupted. When you keep your heart as an open book before the Lord, every time you recognize a need, you continue the conversation and ask God for his input. He delights in answering us right where we are. Wisdom is found in choosing to live today to the fullest.

Pray for today's grace and remain open to receive it throughout your day.

A GENTLE APPROACH

Have nothing to do with foolish, ignorant controversies; you know that they breed quarrels. And the Lord's servant must not be quarrelsome but kind to everyone, able to teach, patiently enduring evil, correcting his opponents with gentleness.

2 Timothy 2:23-25 ESV

Let us not, therefore, be prompt in arguments and indolent in prayers.
—St. Augustine, On the Gift of Perseverance

God's Word is not spread by force. It isn't received by winning heated debates. The Word of God is Christ—he is the Living Word. He spoke with authority, but he did not get caught up in arguments that distracted from the core of the gospel message.

He walked in the power of God. He healed the sick and brought freedom to those tormented in their minds. He brought the message of God's peace to all who would listen. Why, then, would we change the message to be the things that take us further from God's heart? Let's be steadfast in prayer, humble in love, and gracious in our approach.

Pray for Christ's grace and gentleness to soften your heart.

IT STARTS WITH US

We do not give up. Even though our outer person is being destroyed, our inner person is being renewed day by day.
2 CORINTHIANS 4:16 CSB

Revival begins by Christians getting right first and then spills over into the world. —C. H. Spurgeon, The Great Revival

The work of God always starts with the inner work. The change doesn't start on the outside. The change we want to see has to begin in us first. The law of God's love says, "Love the Lord your God with all your heart, mind, and soul, and love your neighbor as yourself." The outer change reflects inner transformation all based in God's love.

If we want to see God's love change the world, it has to change us! Let us pray with fervor for God's powerful mercy to penetrate to the deepest parts of us, right through all of the fear, guilt, shame, and worry. Inner renewal is always available!

Ask the Lord to continue the work he has started in you.

WITH EVERY HEARTBEAT

He satisfies the thirsty
and fills up the hungry.
Psalm 107:9 NCV

Prayer is the spiritual pulse of the soul, by which it beats strongly after God. —Thomas Watson, The Godly Man's Picture

God's powerful provision satisfies the thirsty and fills up the hungry. He sustains us with life. He is the reason we live, move, and have our being. May we offer the Lord our continual thanks as we meditate on his power to heal, save, and redeem. A practice of gratitude moves our attention from just getting by to reasons to rejoice.

The more we pray, the more we are apt to pray. Action follows intention, so let's be sure to set the intentions of our heart upon the Lord. Just as we move through the day in our physical bodies, we can know the fellowship of God's grace as we lean on his Spirit moving within us. With every heartbeat, give thanks.

Spend time in gratitude as you pray.

WALK IN HIS WAYS

By this we know that we are in Him: the one who says that he remains in Him ought, himself also, to walk just as He walked.

1 JOHN 2:5-6 NASB

His heart is ever lifted up to God at all times and in all places. In this he is never hindered, much less interrupted, by any person or thing. In retirement or company, in leisure, business, or conversation, his heart is ever with the Lord. Whether he lie down or rise up, God is in all his thoughts; he walks with God continually, having the loving eye of his mind still fixed upon Him, and everywhere "seeing him that is invisible." —John Wesley, The Character of a Methodist

No matter where we are, what we're doing, or who we're around, we can remain rooted in our Savior's presence. Fellowship with God can be as consistent as our breath. When we keep our minds and hearts set on Christ, it is easier to follow his lead. His movements become our movements. His grace flows steadily to strengthen, instruct, and liberate us.

This is what remaining in the vine is like. Our hearts remain an open book before the Lord: the ears and eyes of our hearts listening and watching for the Spirit.

Keep your heart open before the Lord and listen for his voice.

FURTHERING FAITH

Faith comes from hearing, that is, hearing the Good News about Christ.
ROMANS 10:17 NLT

The greater the difficulty to be overcome, the more will it be seen to the glory of God how much can be done by prayer and faith.
—George Müller, Narratives

Keeping our minds set on the Word of the Lord will keep our thoughts directed by God's gracious leadership. If we want our faith to grow, we have to stretch our comfort levels. It is good news when we have challenges we don't know how to overcome. God is able, and he will strengthen us as we rely on him.

Reliance on God does not mean inactivity. It means obedience. The more you rely on God, the more you will be compelled to walk in the ways of Christ. His good news is exceedingly good for everyone who believes.

Ask God to reframe your challenge in the light of his grace and faithfulness.

HOPEFUL PATIENCE

If we hope for what we do not see, we eagerly wait for it with perseverance.
Romans 8:25 NKJV

God in heaven will hear your prayers, and will answer them. He has never failed, if a man has been honest in his petitions and honest in his confessions. Let your faith beget patience. God is never in a hurry, said St. Augustine, because He has all eternity to work.
—D. L. Moody, Prevailing Prayer

Many of us would rather move swiftly than be told to be patient and wait. Waiting requires patience, and even more, endurance. In the space between asking for God's help and receiving his answer, there is opportunity to delight ourselves in the grace of God.

Waiting can be uncomfortable especially at first. But there is beauty in waiting. God is faithful, and he will do all that he has promised. He isn't in a hurry, and it's not to frustrate you. He wants you to know the power of his presence in the waiting and in the victory. Learn to cultivate contentment in unknowns, and you will have the power of God's peace in every circumstance.

Ask the Lord to teach you how to wait well.

STRAIGHT TO THE HEART

"Do not consider his appearance or his height, for I have rejected him. The Lord does not look at the things people look at. People look at the outward appearance, but the Lord looks at the heart."

1 Samuel 16:7 NIV

Desires are the soul and life of prayer; words are but the body; now as the body without the soul is dead, so are prayers unless they are animated with our desires. —Thomas Watson, The Godly Man's Picture

Prayers without heart are empty. They are prayed out of duty or show, and they aren't based in what is true—what we truly desire or need. A heart can pray without words.

While we may be impressed by pretty words or shows of piety, God is not distracted from the most important element: the heart. When Samuel went looking for the next king in Jesse's household, he was met with many good-looking options. The Lord didn't need men with brawn, he wanted a man after his heart. That's why he chose David. Let's remember the most important element of our prayers: the posture and intentions of our heart.

Ask the Lord to look at your heart and show you what he sees.

ALWAYS PRAY

He told them a parable to the effect that they ought always to pray and not lose heart.
LUKE 18:1 ESV

God commands men to pray, and so not to pray is plain disobedience to an imperative command of Almighty God.
—E. M. Bounds, The Weapon of Prayer

Jesus taught his disciples to pray and not lose heart. There isn't a situation so hard or an obstacle too large that we should not bring it before the Lord in prayer. Often, God changes our perspective about it by meeting us with the presence of his peace in the moment. We can trust him to lead us to breakthrough. He is our victory, and it is in his name that we move.

It is also in Christ's name that we pray. Jesus did not just say, "It would be really good if you prayed. You need it." He set the example by taking time to pray often and many times alone. He needed prayer, and so do we. As we pray, we align our hearts with his and receive the strength we need for each day.

Ask the Lord to help you remember his words and experience the courage you need.

A SWEET LIFE

Live a life of love just as Christ loved us and gave himself for us as a sweet-smelling offering and sacrifice to God.
Ephesians 5:2 NCV

O God, of Thy goodness give me Thyself, for Thou art enough for me, and I may ask nothing that is less and find any full honors to Thee. God give me Thyself! —Julian of Norwich, Revelations of Divine Love

It is no small thing to experience the love of God. It is the essence of his being and the satisfying nourishment we need. When we ask to have more of God, we ask for his fullness: the greatest, most substantial gift that keeps on giving. There is no end to his love, and there is no cap on his peace. All that we could imagine, and so much more, is available in his generous person.

The more we get of God, the more we see at every turn that it is his love that matters most. Living a life of love is our sacrifice of praise poured out each day. Choosing kindness over revenge, patience over anger, and understanding over pushing our opinions are all expressions of love.

What of God is an expression you want more of in your life? Ask him for it.

PRAY FOR THEM

I know this will lead to my salvation through your prayers and help from the Spirit of Jesus Christ.
PHILIPPIANS 1:19 CSB

It is in intercession for others that our faith and love and perseverance will be aroused, and that power of the Spirit be found which can fit us for saving men. —Andrew Murray, The Ministry of Intercession

Intercession is a gift to our spiritual life. As we pray for others, lifting them up, our hearts are stirred in God's presence. It doesn't remain in the realm of what we feel on a human level. God is able to transform our hearts for other people as we pray for them and move in their lives in answer to prayer.

How often do you pray for other people? Instead of feeling guilty, use this as an opportunity to stretch your comfort level. Set a timer for ten minutes, and spend that whole time praying for other people—whoever comes to mind. God can do so much through our prayers. Let's give him the opportunity to do it!

Be intentional about praying for others today.

COME TOGETHER

All these were continually devoting themselves with one mind to prayer.
Acts 1:14 NASB

In the hour of darkest portent, when the case of the church, local or universal, has seemed beyond hope, believing men and believing women have met together and cried to God and the answer has come.
—R. A. Torrey, How to Pray

After Jesus ascended, his followers continued to meet together in prayer. It was in one such meeting that the Holy Spirit fell on them. When we devote ourselves to pray and seek God's face together, he responds with the power of his presence.

When times are tough, let's not just sit back and talk about it. Let's gather with other believers and pray for God to move. With him is the breakthrough we need. In him is the strength we require. What a gift it is to come together in community and pray together for God to come through in faithfulness. He does not fail to answer.

Gather with others in prayer this week.

IN HIS NAME

"You can ask for anything in my name, and I will do it, so that the Son can bring glory to the Father."
JOHN 14:13 NLT

When you plead the name of Christ, you plead that which shakes the gates of hell and that which the hosts of heaven obey, and God Himself feels the sacred power of that divine plea.
—C. H. Spurgeon, Order and Argument in Prayer

At the name of Jesus every knee will bow, and every tongue confess that he is Lord. His name is high and lifted up: high above every other name. It is the name where we find our authority as his people. It is in his name that we pray, and by his power that we live in the freedom of his love.

When our hearts are yielded to Christ and we seek to follow him, we can ask him anything and he will do it. If it brings glory to the Father, he will answer your prayer in power. Let us not hold back from praying in his name for souls to be freed, lives to be saved, and peace to pervade our families, cities, and nations.

Pray in Jesus' name for powerful breakthrough.

NEVER FORSAKEN

I have been young, and now am old;
Yet I have not seen the righteous forsaken,
Nor his descendants begging bread.
PSALM 37:25 NKJV

Of His bounty, the Lord often grants not what we seek, so as to bestow something preferable. —St. Augustine, The Three Greatest Prayers

God's generosity is boundless. He doesn't always answer our prayers in the ways we expect, but he is faithful to answer in a way that we couldn't imagine. Oftentimes, his answers astound us with how thoughtful he is. His ways are better, his thoughts higher, and his clarity truer than ours. He knows every factor to consider.

We can trust God to meet us with gracious generosity. Let's loosen our expectations over specific details and allow the Lord to work as he will. We see in part and know in part, but he sees everything fully. We can trust his hand, but much more than that, we can trust his heart. He never leaves his people begging for bread. He supplies what we need.

Ask the Lord to show you how he has creatively answered prayers that you missed.

A DIFFERENT WAY

"If the world hates you, keep in mind that it hated me first."
JOHN 15:18 NIV

Prayer is the safest method of replying to a word of hatred.
—C. H. Spurgeon, Morning and Evening

Though many loved Jesus, people in power hated him. There were many offended by his message of peace, love, and salvation for all who believe. Jesus broke down the false notion that God only tolerated us. He fulfilled the law and did away with perfectionism. He offered grace in its place. This is the way of God, and it is much more gracious than many are willing to believe or receive, even those who consider themselves religious.

How do we become more like the Lord? We follow his lead. Did he respond in kind when people hated him? Did he humiliate those who mocked him? Did he yell God's judgment over those who misunderstood him? Pray for the patience, kindness, and mercy of the Lord, and walk it out.

Instead of lashing out in defense, pray for those who hate you, hurt you, or misunderstand you.

SONS AND DAUGHTERS

You are no longer a slave, but a son, and if a son, then an heir through God.

GALATIANS 4:7 ESV

The law of prayer, the right to pray, rests on sonship.
—E. M. Bounds, The Necessity of Prayer

There is nothing keeping you from reaching out to the Lord today. If he is your Father, why would you stay at a distance? Have you felt distant from his heart lately? Ashamed of choices you've made? It's a perfect time to reacquaint yourself with the overwhelming mercy of God through the parable of the prodigal son in Luke 15.

No matter if you have stayed close to your Father's house, or if you have wandered, there is no reason to doubt his loving reception of you. He delights in his children, and he longs for them to be with him. Go to him now, and receive the embrace of his welcome once more.

Let your prayers lead you home to your loving Father.

LEAN INTO LOVE

Where God's love is, there is no fear, because God's perfect love drives out fear. It is punishment that makes a person fear, so love is not made perfect in the person who fears.
1 JOHN 4:18 NCV

Prayer will make a man cease from sin, or sin will entice a man to cease from prayer. —John Bunyan, Mr. John Bunyan's Dying Sayings

If we want to live more rightly, loving others as God loves us, we have to stay connected to the heart of the Father through prayer. The more we seek him, the more we find him. The more we ask for his help, the more we receive it willingly.

There is no fear or shame in God's presence. His love drives it out, covering us fully in the light of his powerful redemption. Fear of punishment can keep us from connecting with God. Thinking it's better to go our own way and sin will keep us from prayer. Let us press into the love of God, for there our hearts are renewed and empowered.

Is there anything keeping you from going to the Lord? Let his love lead you and drive away your fear.

OVERJOYED

How joyful is the one
whose transgression is forgiven,
whose sin is covered!
PSALM 32:1 CSB

Daily bread may make us live comfortably but forgiveness of sins will make us die comfortably. —Thomas Watson, The Lord's Prayer

In God's grace, we do not have to choose between his provision and salvation. It is all a reflection of his incredible mercy and power. Those who are forgiven much, and feel the weight of their debts lifted off, have much reason to rejoice. We have our daily bread, but what's better is that we have eternal salvation in Jesus Christ.

If it's been a while since you've thanked the Lord for all he has done for you, for the gracious forgiveness of your sins and the liberation you receive in his love, spend some time in prayer thanking him. Rejoice in the Lord, for not only is he your provider, but he is also your powerful redeemer!

Pour out your heartfelt thanks to God and let the joy of your relief bubble over in praise.

AS IT IS IN HEAVEN

"Your kingdom come.
Your will be done,
On earth as it is in heaven."
MATTHEW 6:10 NASB

I think we shall find a great many of our prayers that we thought unanswered answered when we get to heaven.
—D. L. Moody, Prevailing Prayer

God does not work according to our timelines. Though this may feel frustrating at times, he always knows what he is doing. We may not see the ways in which he faithfully follows through, but he always does.

We see a tiny portion of what is going on, but God sees it all. Let's not lose hope when we don't see the promises of God as we expect them to come. Let's instead ask for eyes to see and ears to hear. Let's offer the Lord our sacrifice of praise and trust that all will be revealed in the fullness of time, even if it's when we stand before the Lord in eternity.

Pray for God's kingdom, plan, and purposes to be done on earth as it is in heaven. Choose trust when you cannot see how he will come through.

CHRIST'S GREATEST OFFERING

That is why, when Christ came into the world, he said to God,
"You did not want animal sacrifices or sin offerings.
But you have given me a body to offer."
HEBREWS 10:5 NLT

The praying of Jesus Christ drew on the mightiest forces of His being. His prayers were His sacrifices, which He offered before He offered Himself on the cross for the sins of mankind. Prayer-sacrifice is the forerunner and pledge of self-sacrifice. —E. M. Bounds, The Reality of Prayer

Christ's greatest offering was the sacrifice of his body as the Son of God. Before he sacrificed his life, though, he sacrificed his time, attention, and heart. He stayed connected to his Father through prayer and obedience. If we want to walk in the ways of Jesus, we cannot skip to the end of our own stories. We have to make sacrifices each day.

Prayer keeps us connected to our God and King. Our hearts are transformed in his presence, and we grow in grace, stature, and wisdom as we take each step. We cannot be so focused on where we're going that we miss the ways to cultivate connection, growth, character, and movement today.

Pray to the Lord and ask him to reveal what you're responsibility is to follow through on today.

WHATEVER YOU DO

Whether you eat or drink, or whatever you do, do all to the glory of God.

1 CORINTHIANS 10:31 NKJV

When we are living for the Lord and living to please and honor Him, eating our breakfast can be just as spiritual as having our family prayers. —A.W. Tozer, The Pursuit of God

We so often separate into categories what God sees as one. It does not matter what we are doing, whether serving, working, or eating our breakfast. If we are living connected to the Lord and submitted to his leadership, even the most mundane things are sacred.

Brother Lawrence, a monk assigned with doing the dishes, put everything he had into that simple, ordinary task and it became to him the most sacred act he could offer. This is what each of us is invited to do. Let's invite the power of God's presence into the mundane and ordinary as we turn our hearts to him in praise and do our work diligently for his glory.

What ordinary task will you make sacred through your heart posture today?

NATURAL OVERFLOW

May the Lord make your love increase and overflow for each other and for everyone else, just as ours does for you.
1 THESSALONIANS 3:12 NIV

Prayer is the natural outgushing of a soul in communion with Jesus. Just as the leaf and the fruit will come out of the vine-branch without any conscious effort on the part of the branch, but simply because of its living union with the stem, so prayer buds, and blossoms, and fruits out of souls abiding in Jesus.
—C. H. Spurgeon, Prayer and Spiritual Warfare

Abide in the Lord, and your heart will grow, blossom, and thrive in his love. We do not make the fruit of the Spirit appear in our lives. It is a natural outflow of our surrender to the care and leadership of our Savior.

We may do our best, but God's grace is even better. He partners with our efforts and fills us with strength in our weakness so our love will increase and overflow in practical ways. Love is not a limited resource, and neither is peace, joy, faith, or hope. There is always more. Let us remain connected to the vine, and our lives will be a natural overflow of his goodness.

How connected are you to the Lord on a daily basis?

MUSIC TO HIS EARS

Oh sing to the Lord a new song;
sing to the Lord, all the earth!
Sing to the Lord, bless his name;
tell of his salvation from day to day.
Psalm 96:1-2 ESV

He who sings prays twice.
—St. Augustine, Expositions on the Book of Psalms

Prayer does not have to be limited to spoken prayers. If we can live our prayers, we can certainly sing them too. How often do you engage in worship through song? Music is powerful and has the ability to go beyond logic to the realm of spirit, soul, and heart.

Sing to the Lord a new song, or at the very least sing to the Lord a song that reflects your desire for him. Whether it's a hymn, popular praise song, or a melody that you make up on the spot, sing your heart out to the Lord in your personal prayer time today. It doesn't matter if you like your voice or not. It's all music to his ears, and he delights in your voice as it lifts to him!

Sing a song as a prayerful offering to the Lord today.

EVERLASTING TRUTH

Every word of God is pure;
He is a shield to those who put their trust in Him.
PROVERBS 30:5 NKJV

God's Word is pure and sure, in spite of the devil, in spite of your fear, in spite of everything.
—R. A. Torrey, The Power of Prayer and the Prayer of Power

It doesn't matter what comes against the Word of God—whether it's the powers of this world, our own fear, or doubt—it stands the test of time. The living expression of God's Word is Christ. He is the revelation of the Father's heart in flesh and bones, and his Word is the one we can confidently bind our lives to.

When we stand upon the Word in prayer, we can rest assured that what the Lord promises, he will do. Isaiah 55:11 assures, "[the words I speak] will not return to me empty. They make the things happen that I want to happen, and they succeed in doing what I send them to do." God's Word will never return void. They accomplish his will, so why wouldn't we join our prayers to his everlasting truth?

Pray from Scripture today.

EVIDENT MERCY

Bearing with one another and forgiving one another if anyone has a grievance against another. Just as the Lord has forgiven you, so you are also to forgive.
COLOSSIANS 3:13 CSB

Our forgiving love toward men is the evidence of God's forgiving love in us. It is a necessary condition of the prayer of faith.
—Andrew Murray, With Christ in the School of Prayer

If our witness of faith falls short of mercy that forgives others, let us realign ourselves with the law of God's love. We have been forgiven, so who are we to withhold it from others? Instead of holding grudges against one another, let's learn to lean in with love.

It's counter-cultural to do this. While others shout, demean, and grow bitter against those who disagree with them, let's choose the narrow path: the path of Christ's mercy. His example becomes our measure. What he forgave, certainly so can we. We can choose to open our hearts in grace, and ask for the Spirit to empower us to love when we'd rather ridicule. Where we fall short, God stands ready and tall to help us in our weakness.

Pray for grace to bear with those who you disagree with and forgive each other as Christ forgave you.

HIGHER GROUND

If you have been raised with Christ, keep seeking the things that are above, where Christ is, seated at the right hand of God. Set your minds on the things that are above, not on the things that are on earth.

COLOSSIANS 3:1-2 NASB

My heart has no desire to stay Where doubts arise and fears dismay; Though some may dwell where these abound, My prayer, my aim, is higher ground. —Johnson Oatman, Jr., Higher Ground

Prayer keeps us reaching for the things that are above and beyond our perception. It raises up to the perspective of Christ, where he sits at the right hand of the Father. When we set our minds on what is above, we learn to let go of the things we cannot control and take hold of the grace God offers.

Are you worried? Afraid? Filled with doubts? Don't be ashamed; rather turn your attention to the higher ground of God through prayer. Ask to see from his heavenly perspective. It is from a higher vantage that everything is put into perspective. What seems weighty and confusing is clarified from a bird's eye view. This is what prayer can do: raise us up with Christ so that we can rest in trust.

Pray for a higher perspective of your troubles.

WORKING IN PRAYER

Work hard so you can present yourself to God and receive his approval. Be a good worker, one who does not need to be ashamed and who correctly explains the word of truth.

2 TIMOTHY 2:15 NLT

Prayer is the keynote of the most sanctified life, of the holiest ministry. He does the most for God who is the highest skilled in prayer.
—E. M. Bounds, Power Through Prayer

Everything you do will be made better by persistent prayer. If you want to do good work and stay on the path of God's love, you'll need to rely on his presence each day. What else will prepare you to do that, or connect you to his direct leadership, better than a prayerfully surrendered heart?

Let prayer be the keynote of your life. Begin your day with it, and end it with thanks. Use every opportunity you have to reach out to the Lord throughout your day. It might feel like work to start, but it will become a most sacred habit that keeps you open, alert, and submitted to the heart of the Father.

Ask the Lord to help you build a strong practice of prayer, and to show you how he works through it.

RUN TOWARD THE LORD

Oh, satisfy us early with Your mercy,
That we may rejoice and be glad all our days!
Psalm 90:14 NKJV

He who runs from God in the morning will scarcely find Him the rest of the day. —John Bunyan, A Discourse Touching Prayer

As we pray, we turn our attention to the Lord. It can be with words on our lips, but it can also be in the place of our thoughts. Our hearts, even, can open before him, welcoming him in with nary a word, but a gesture of invitation.

What do you give your attention to? Let your heart's undercurrent be like a river of continual connection to the Father. You don't have to always be actively thinking of God to come back to him over and over again. When you begin your day by running to him, you will rejoice and be glad, finding him where he meets you throughout your day.

Begin your day with an open heart and invitation for the Lord to meet you in the ordinary.

SPIRITUAL POWER

The weapons we fight with are not the weapons of the world. On the contrary, they have divine power to demolish strongholds. We demolish arguments and every pretension that sets itself up against the knowledge of God, and we take captive every thought to make it obedient to Christ.

2 Corinthians 10:4-5 NIV

Those who have left the deepest impression on this sin-cursed earth have been men and women of prayer. —D. L. Moody, Prevailing Prayer

The weapons of the Spirit are not the weapons of this world. We don't take down our enemies by force, but we extend love that breaks down barriers. The way of the Cross seems foolish to those who haven't received the power of God's love in their lives. But to those of us who have been liberated by love? We remain grateful and our hearts ready to follow the ways of Christ.

When we are tempted to fight those around us, let's turn instead to prayer. It can do much more in connection to God's presence than our mere words to others can. Prayer also keeps our hearts ready to change when there is hardness. Spiritual power is found not in enlightenment, but in surrender to the Lord and his love.

When you want to fight with others, remember your only mandate is to love, and turn your angst into prayers.

ENDEAVOR TO LOVE

Put away all malice and all deceit and hypocrisy and envy and all slander.
1 PETER 2:1 ESV

A godly man will forgive those who have wronged him... Though I would not trust an enemy—yet I would endeavor to love him. I would exclude him from my creed—but not from my prayer.
—Thomas Watson, The Godly Man's Picture

Choosing to forgive those who wrong us doesn't mean that we blindly trust them. We release them, extending love, and that love can be the space put between us. We trust God, our faithful Father. We trust people of integrity and love, those who are honest, true, and dependable.

Prayerfully, we endeavor to love all people, and Jesus himself helps us in that aim. When we forgive, we choose God's love over our own disappointment, hate, or fear. Forgiveness does not mean being okay with how things went. It doesn't rewrite history. It clears the slate of the present and future. Endeavoring to love is our call in Christ.

Can you try to love those you struggle to forgive? Ask the Lord to help you.

ETERNALLY SIGHTED

We are surrounded by a great cloud of people whose lives tell us what faith means. So let us run the race that is before us and never give up. We should remove from our lives anything that would get in the way and the sin that so easily holds us back.

Hebrews 12:1 NCV

Lord, stamp eternity on my eyeballs.
—Jonathan Edwards, The Life and Diary of David Brainerd

When we set our eyes of faith on the Lord, we step outside of the realm of time. Though we live in this body, in this place and age, our vision does not end with our physical sight. We know we are living for more than this frail existence.

Ecclesiastes 3:11 says, God "has set eternity in the human heart." Our hearts are already turned toward what lies beyond the veil. Still, Edwards takes it a step further to ask God to stamp it on his eyeballs. Oh, that we would have eyes to see so that we wouldn't stumble over the pebbles of worry, mistrust, or offense in our path.

Set your sights on eternity in your prayers today.

GLORIFY HIS NAME

So that you may approve the things that are superior and may be pure and blameless in the day of Christ.

PHILIPPIANS 1:10 CSB

The glory we give God is nothing else but our lifting up his name in the world, and magnifying him in the eyes of others. Christ shall be magnified in my body. —Thomas Watson, Divine Cordial

If we want to lift high the name of Jesus in our lives, it starts with glorifying him in our hearts. Spend time in prayer, worship, and reading his Word. The more we know him, the more we love him. The more we love him, the more we want to know him.

Your personal prayer time is sacred. It is a direct connection to God, and no one can disrupt or keep you from it. Set your heart on the Lord, lift up his name in your own time, and it will become natural to do it with others. Don't worry about getting from where you are to where you want to be in Christ. Take each step, starting at home, and trust the journey.

Prioritize time in prayer to lift high the name of Jesus in your own life.

CHRIST'S LIFE IN YOU

I have been crucified with Christ; and it is no longer I who live, but Christ lives in me; and the life which I now live in the flesh I live by faith in the Son of God, who loved me and gave Himself up for me.

Galatians 2:20 NASB

Faith has no desire to have its own will, when that will is not in accordance with the mind of God; for such a desire would at bottom be the impulse of an unbelief which did not rely upon God's judgment as our best guide. Faith knows that God's will is the highest good, and that anything which is beneficial to us will be granted to our petitions.
—D. L. Moody, Prevailing Prayer

When we surrender our lives to Christ, the Spirit of God takes up residence in our hearts. Christ becomes the source of our strength, the lifeblood of our existence. As we pair our life with Christ, his love draws us into deeper communion. We have everything we need in the fountain of his grace.

When we pray, it's okay to begin with what we want, but let's not leave it there. Even Jesus prayed for the cup to be taken from him. But he yielded his will to the Father's. Let's follow his example and do the same.

Allow space in your prayers for God to have his way.

PERSISTENT PEACE

"I have told you all this so that you may have peace in me. Here on earth you will have many trials and sorrows. But take heart, because I have overcome the world."

JOHN 16:33 NLT

We can do nothing without prayer. All things can be done by importunate prayer. It surmounts or removes all obstacles, overcomes every resisting force and gains its ends in the face of invincible hindrances. —E. M. Bounds, The Weapon of Prayer

Prayer is powerful. It opens us up to receive what Christ has already promised us. When we're feeling fearful, let us turn our hearts in prayer to the one who promised peace that passes understanding. He has already overcome the world, and he can just as easily overcome our hearts in present peace.

We face many obstacles, but the presence of God is always with us. We never go into the battles of life alone. God has the solutions we need, the strength we lack, and the wisdom to get through. And through all of this, he offers us the peace of his love to steady us.

Pray for God's persistent peace to rule in your heart today.

TRUSTWORTHY FATHER

"Go and learn what this means: 'I desire mercy and not sacrifice.' For I did not come to call the righteous, but sinners, to repentance."

Matthew 9:13 NKJV

Wherever faith has accepted the Father's love, obedience accepts the Father's will. The surrender to, and the prayer for a life of heaven-like obedience, is the spirit of childlike prayer.
—Andrew Murray, With Christ in the School of Prayer

The more we experience the love of God, the easier it is to follow his ways. His love expands our understanding. It breaks down the walls of fear, shame, and every excuse to limit his mercy.

Obedience is not a dirty word. It is the loving reaction to a trustworthy Father. The longer we walk with the Lord in submission, the more readily we trust him because he has been tested and found faithful in our lives. He doesn't expect perfection from us, just willingness to try. As he corrects us and redirects us, we learn to trust him more with every step.

Pray for heaven-like obedience to God's ways.

POWER FOLLOWS PRAYER

Is anyone among you sick? Let them call the elders of the church to pray over them and anoint them with oil in the name of the Lord. And the prayer offered in faith will make the sick person well; the Lord will raise them up. If they have sinned, they will be forgiven.

James 5:14-15 NIV

If we would spend more nights before God on our faces in prayer, there would be more days of power when we faced our people!
—R. A. Torrey, The Power of Prayer and the Prayer of Power

If we want to experience the power of God's miraculous mercy in our lives—his restorative, healing, breakthrough power—it begins by prayer. Prayers of faith are not needed when the provision is simple. They are needed when we don't have an easy solution. This is where we invite God's power to move, and to make the impossible a reality.

Taking our problems to God is a good practice. Doing it in fellowship with others? A powerful one. Let's not neglect the beautiful gift of communal prayer and petition.

Invite others into a need you cannot see the provision for by asking them to pray with you.

BECOME FAMILIAR

All Scripture is breathed out by God and profitable for teaching, for reproof, for correction, and for training in righteousness, that the man of God may be complete, equipped for every good work.

2 TIMOTHY 3:16-17 ESV

The best praying man is the man who is most believingly familiar with the promises of God. After all, prayer is nothing but taking God's promises to him, and saying to him, "Do as thou hast said." Prayer is the promise utilized. A prayer which is not based on a promise has no true foundation. —C. H. Spurgeon, Prayer and Spiritual Warfare

The more acquainted we are with the Word of God, the more powerful our prayers become, because they are infused with the truth of who he is.

The promises of God are a sure foundation for our prayer life. Time spent studying and meditating on Scripture is never wasted. The Spirit breathes on our understanding and brings to mind the right word at the right time.

Spend time in God's Word today and pray a promise of Scripture.

He Sees

The Lord sees everything you do,
and he watches where you go.
Proverbs 5:21 NCV

It is a wicked prayer to ask to have someone to hate or to fear, so that he may be someone to conquer. —St. Augustine, The City of God

Scripture tells us the eye of the Lord searches to find those who are completely submitted to him (2 Chronicles 16:9). He watches over us and looks at our hearts. He cannot be tricked or manipulated. When we pray out of fear or bitterness toward another, the answer to our prayer becomes what he does in our own hearts. He is love, and he moves in mercy and truth always.

If our desire is to better ourselves by belittling others, God will not act on our behalf. It goes against his very nature. He is not a man that he would lie, and he is not fooled by the duplicity of charismatic liars. What he does, he does well.

Pray for a humble heart and love that expands your own borders rather than limits them.

AUTHENTIC PRAYERS

How long, LORD? Will you forget me forever?
How long will you hide your face from me?
How long will I store up anxious concerns within me,
agony in my mind every day?
PSALM 13:1-2 CSB

Not to pray because you do not feel fit to pray is like saying, "I will not take medicine because I am too ill." Pray for prayer: pray yourself, by the Spirit's assistance, into a praying frame.
—C. H. Spurgeon, Prayer and Spiritual Warfare

When we don't feel like praying, that's the place we begin. The psalms are filled with the breadth of the human experience. In today's verse, we see an example of someone who probably didn't feel like praying to begin with, but he poured out his authentic feelings before the Lord.

God's not afraid of your honesty. He welcomes it. He meets you just as you are, and you don't have to pretend to be anything different. When you don't feel like praying, let that be your starting point.

Don't pray what you think God wants to hear; pray from the reality of where you're at today.

A NEW NAME

You will be called by a new name
Which the mouth of the LORD will designate.
ISAIAH 62:2 NASB

If I bear the name of another, I have given up my own name and my own independent life.
—Andrew Murray, With Christ in the School of Prayer

When we come to God through Christ, he offers us a new name. We are no longer identified by our past. He gives us his name. We are welcomed into his family, and we take on the rights of sons and daughters.

The children of God all share the inheritance of his kingdom. No longer can the guilt of our past be held against us. No more is the fear, shame, and sin of our youth what we are known by. As far as the east is from the west, that's how far he's removed our transgressions from us. We are known as his children, and the authority of his name carries a heavier weight than we can imagine.

Thank God for giving you a new name—his name—and the confidence of being his child.

MEDITATE

I recall all you have done, O LORD;
I remember your wonderful deeds of long ago.
They are constantly in my thoughts.
I cannot stop thinking about your mighty works.
PSALM 77:11-12 NLT

Spend some time, maybe a week or a day on each of the following attributes or perfections of God and on how they affect your prayer life: His self-sufficiency, omniscience, sovereignty, goodness, omnipotence, omnipresence, immutability, wisdom, holiness, love, grace, righteousness, justice, and mercy.
—A.W. Tozer, The Knowledge of the Holy

It is a beautiful practice to take an attribute of the Lord and meditate on it for a while. When we think about God's justice, and how it will never be compromised, and we remember his mercy that cannot be quenched, the Spirit reveals deeper understanding of who God is and how he moves.

What attribute of God do you want more understanding of? Which do you hunger most for at this time? Write it down in a place you can see it, maybe on a post it note on your desk, the dashboard of your car, or your bathroom mirror. Each time you see it, meditate on who God is and ask him to reveal the power of that to you in greater ways.

Pray for deeper revelation of the power of God's being.

WITH A WORD

Then God said, "Let there be light"; and there was light.
GENESIS 1:3 NKJV

There may be no sign of it, no probability of it, no germ of it from which to start, but God is able to make it out of nothing by a word. He does so make it by the word which faith claims. He needs no protoplasm to build His magnificent edifices of worlds. "He spake, and it was done; He commanded, and it stood fast." Into the soul that has no basis or remnant of goodness, but is dead in trespasses and sins, He can speak life and holiness. —A.B. Simpson, Standing on Faith

God is the one who created light out of darkness by speaking it into existence. He does not need our help to do a thing! Still, he delights in partnering with his people and moving in response to their prayers.

If nothing is impossible with God, remember, too, that no one is out of the reach of his mercy. He can save anyone, anywhere, anytime! Let's never give up hope, for God can speak life and holiness into every single human heart.

Pray for someone you'd given up hope on.

EVERY DAY IN PRAYER

"Be always on the watch, and pray that you may be able to escape all that is about to happen, and that you may be able to stand before the Son of Man."

LUKE 21:36 NIV

The meaning is—not that we should be always praying—but that we should every day set some time apart for prayer.
—Thomas Watson, The Godly Man's Picture

We pray without ceasing, not so that we convince God of anything, but so that we move our hearts in connection to the source of all life. He is our steady peace and strength. Being watchful and praying means we keep not only our hearts ready, but also our eyes upon the Lord in every circumstance.

Being always on the watch doesn't mean our minds never wander. We don't get to opt out of life. We have to feed our families, go to work, and do the mundane things. Let's make time for prayer, even paired with those things, directing our attention to the Son of Man.

Devote at least ten minutes to prayer today.

THE LORD ANSWERS

When Manasseh prayed, the Lord heard him and had pity on him. So the Lord let him return to Jerusalem and to his kingdom. Then Manasseh knew that the Lord is the true God.

2 CHRONICLES 33:13 NCV

Surely if God answered the prayer of wicked Manasseh, he will hear ours in the time of our distress. —D. L. Moody, Prevailing Prayer

Manasseh was not a good man. He was known as the wickedest king of Israel, reversing much of the good his father, King Hezekiah, had instituted. He rebuilt altars to other gods, and sacrificed his children in his pursuit of favor with those gods. God spoke, but he did not listen. It was only when he was captured by the king of Assyria and brought to Babylon that he humbled himself before God in prayer.

From a truly humble and desperate place, Manasseh was able to connect with the God he had ignored all his life. God restored him to his place in the kingdom of Israel. How gracious God was to him!

It's never too late to humble yourself before the Lord. Pray for those who seem irredeemable today.

RIVER OF GRACE

The grace of our Lord overflowed, along with the faith and love that are in Christ Jesus.
1 TIMOTHY 1:14 CSB

By his sacrifice he has made way for grace to run like a river into the world. —John Bunyan, A Discourse Touching Prayer

Grace is like a rushing river, overflowing its banks. When Christ revealed the power of God's love to people through his practical kindness, his wise teachings, and miracles of healing, he broke open the limits we placed on God's mercy.

Through his death and resurrection, Christ broke the power of sin, fear, shame, and death once and for all. He released the abundance, the enormous generosity, of God's grace in the world. We can find it anywhere. Just as we cannot escape the love of God in this world, so too is his grace ever-present.

What do you need grace for today? Ask the Lord and receive from his generous portion.

FAITH-FILLED ACTION

What use is it, my brothers and sisters, if someone says he has faith, but he has no works? Can that faith save him?

JAMES 2:14 NASB

The Christian should work as if all depended upon him, and pray as if it all depended upon God.
—C. H. Spurgeon, Prayer and Spiritual Warfare

When our faith-filled prayers are joined with faith-filled action, there is a beautiful fellowship between trust in the Lord and partnership with him in our lives. It is usually not one or the other. Waiting, even when we are in such a season, does not mean inactivity.

We do what we can with what we can, and we trust God with the rest. Obedience is not stagnant. It puts into practice what we know to do. When we pray to the Lord, we do not often withdraw from the world for an extended time. We pray, and then we move in the direction of that very prayer. God will never fail us, and we can trust him to guide and redirect us.

How can you demonstrate your faith in God's faithfulness today?

PEACE IN THE STORM

Suddenly, a fierce storm struck the lake, with waves breaking into the boat. But Jesus was sleeping. The disciples went and woke him up, shouting, "Lord, save us! We're going to drown!"
MATTHEW 8:24-25 NLT

Most persons after a step of faith are looking for sunny skies and unruffled seas, and when they meet a storm and tempest they are filled with astonishment and perplexity.
—A.B. Simpson, Days of Heaven Upon Earth

When God calls us to trust him, he doesn't mean when all is calm, and it feels easy to do it. Trust is required in the fierce storms of life. Just because we're experiencing turbulence, and even fear, does not mean we have stepped outside of God's leadership. Jesus was with the disciples on the boat on the Sea of Galilee. He was sleeping peacefully while a tempest was causing his followers to question everything.

When you find yourself in the same kind of boat, go to Jesus. Ask him to quiet the storm of your own heart and to reveal the power of his presence in the midst of circumstances outside your control. He speaks to the wind and waves and quiets them.

Ask Jesus for his peace to quiet the storms.

LITTLE MOVEMENTS OF LOVE

Let us not grow weary while doing good, for in due season we shall reap if we do not lose heart.
GALATIANS 6:9 NKJV

We ought not to be weary of doing little things for the love of God, who regards not the greatness of the work, but the love with which it is performed. —Brother Lawrence, The Practice of the Presence of God

When life is overwhelming, the world chaotic, and the demands many, we may be tempted to throw our hands in the air and exclaim, "What's the point?" When the pressures build, we realize how little we can actually control. We try our best, and sometimes that does not feel good enough. But against what standard?

This is the moment to recalibrate our hearts in the love of God. We cannot do everything. In fact, we cannot do much of what we expect. There is no expectation of perfection in God's eyes. All we can do is all we can do. And that is enough to choose little movements of love each day.

When you are weary, ask God to show you small loving acts you can do.

START HERE

Search me, God, and know my heart;
test me and know my anxious thoughts.
See if there is any offensive way in me,
and lead me in the way everlasting.
PSALM 139:23-24 NIV

Every day we should go to Him first, humbly and straightforwardly, and say, "Lord, is there anything in me that is not according to your will, that has not been ordered by you, or that is not entirely given over to you? What would you have me do today?"
—Andrew Murray, The Inner Life

Asking God to search our hearts is a good practice in staying humble, open, and pliable before him. When we seek his leadership in the mornings, he opens our eyes to what we can do the very day we are given to follow his lead.

Do you begin your days in the presence of God? Do you welcome him to search and know your heart, and to reveal anything in it that stands in the way of his love? He is happy to guide you and overjoyed to offer you his wisdom. His light shines on the deepest places and brings warmth, life, and clarity.

Pray the psalmist's prayer to the Lord each morning this week.

CHANGED BY LOVE

"This is the will of my Father, that everyone who looks on the Son and believes in him should have eternal life, and I will raise him up on the last day."

JOHN 6:40 ESV

God will not compromise and He need not be coaxed. He cannot be persuaded to alter His Word nor talked into answering selfish prayer. In all our efforts to find God, to please Him, to commune with Him, we should remember that all change must be on our part. "I am the Lord, I change not." —A.W. Tozer, The Attributes of God

The transformative power of God's love cannot be measured. It is greater than our resistance, but our willingness aids the process of our unfolding. Flowers bloom in the wild of the field, and our hearts come alive in the presence of God's grace.

Look to the Son today, and live. Let your prayer be one of open-hearted trust. Invite the Holy Spirit to shift what needs to be shifted in order to live in the freedom of Christ's love. We cannot control God, and we don't need to! He is lavish in grace, perfect in love, and always close to those who seek him.

Invite the transformative power of God's love to change your heart and mind in ways that align with his character.

PRESENT JOY

You will teach me how to live a holy life.
Being with you will fill me with joy;
at your right hand I will find pleasure forever.
PSALM 16:11 NCV

It is better to let the work go by default than to let the praying go by neglect. —E. M. Bounds, Power Through Prayer

Time in prayer is never wasted, nor is time spent fixing our eyes on the Lord with heartfelt adoration. As we look to the Son, his light infuses our souls with strength. There is work enough to do every day, and not all of it is urgent.

May you have the grace to let things go when they don't need to be done in the moment. May you embrace each opportunity to experience peace, joy, love, and hope in the fellowship of Christ and with others. There are times to buckle down and get the work done, and there are also times to let it go and embrace what your heart needs in the moment. How willing are you to let the non-urgent go in order to embrace the beauty of this moment?

Let yourself revel in the peace, the power, and the grace of God's love as you turn your heart to him today.

SURE PROVISION

God is able to make every grace overflow to you, so that in every way, always having everything you need, you may excel in every good work.

2 Corinthians 9:8 CSB

He did not of course expect God to create gold and silver and put them into his hands. He knew, however, that God could incline the hearts of men to aid him, and he believed, if the thing that he attempted was of Him, that he would so incline them, in answer to prayer, as his necessities should require. —George Müller, Narratives

God is our good Father and faithful provider. He is able to make every grace overflow to us, so that in every way, always having everything we need, we may excel in every good work. What a powerful promise for us to stand on!

When we don't know where our provision will come from, let's lean into the power of God's faithful promises. He will not let his children beg for bread, for he provides them with the nourishment they need. He will care for our needs as he cares for the birds, the flowers of the field, and the sheep of his pasture. He will always provide a way.

Release your worries of the unknowns of tomorrow, and ask for the peace of God's love to settle your heart in trust.

WALK WITH THE WISE

One who walks with wise people will be wise,
But a companion of fools will suffer harm.
Proverbs 13:20 NASB

Be often among the godly. They are the salt of the earth—and will help to season you. Their counsel may direct you; their prayers may enliven you. Such holy sparks may be thrown into your breasts as may kindle devotion in you. It is good to be among the saints, to learn the trade of godliness. —Thomas Watson, The Godly Man's Picture

Jesus said that we are the salt of the earth. That kind of seasoning is what we need in life. When we walk among the wise, we are seasoned by their wisdom. It is a beautiful reflection of God's transformative wisdom at work in our lives.

How much time do you spend with those who enrich your life? The people who challenge, uplift, and encourage you should be treasured. Honesty and integrity are attributes of the wise. So are grace and kindness. The more we become like God, the more we offer his light to others.

What is the fruit of the company you keep? Ask the Lord for his perspective.

LIFE-GIVING LEADERSHIP

Let the Holy Spirit guide your lives. Then you won't be doing what your sinful nature craves.

GALATIANS 5:16 NLT

Prayer is the key that opens heaven; the favors we ask descend upon us the very instant our prayers ascend to God. —St. Augustine, On Prayer

What a wonderful gift it is to know that we have access to the Creator of all life through the key of prayer. We go to Christ as our mediator, and he welcomes us into the throne room of the Father. The Holy Spirit is our ever-present help, counselor, and guide.

The Spirit's work in our lives is transformative. When we pray, the Spirit guides our prayers to the ears of the Father, and brings the answers and provision through his presence. There is so much more at work than our eyes see, minds comprehend, or hearts know. This is exceedingly good news!

Ask the Holy Spirit to guide your steps today.

SPIRIT WINDS

Suddenly there came a sound from heaven, as of a rushing mighty wind, and it filled the whole house where they were sitting.
ACTS 2:2 NKJV

True prayer is the trading of the heart with God, and the heart never comes into spiritual commerce with the ports of heaven until God the Holy Spirit puts wind into the sails and speeds the ship into its haven.
—C. H. Spurgeon, Prayer and Spiritual Warfare

In the book of Acts, the upper room was where the believers were gathered in prayer. A mighty rushing wind came upon them, and the Holy Spirit filled the entire space. You might know how this continues, with supernatural signs and wonders.

When the wind of the Spirit blows, there is power. There is refreshing, and there is momentum. We cannot bend the Spirit to our will. He moves as God intends. Still, prayer is a powerful way to prepare our hearts for the Spirit's move. Let's trade our hearts with God, offering him all that are in this moment, and trust him to show up and put wind in the sails of our faith.

Whatever time you spend in prayer today, open your heart to the presence and power of the Spirit.

WILLING OBEDIENCE

"I am the Lord's servant," Mary answered. "May your word to me be fulfilled."
LUKE 1:38 NIV

The heart of obedience is in the will, the essence of obedience is the surrender of the will to God. It is going to God our heavenly Father and saying, "Heavenly Father, here I am. I am Thy property. Thou hast bought me with a price. I acknowledge Thine ownership, and surrender myself and all that I am absolutely to Thee. Send me where Thou wilt; do with me what Thou wilt; use me as Thou wilt."
—R. A. Torrey, The Power of Prayer and the Prayer of Power

Obedience is in the follow-through of our actions, but our attitude toward it can differ. Some are reluctant to obey what they know is best, and they do it out of resentment. Some look for ways to do the bare minimum. Others willingly surrender their own fears, opinions, and hesitations and obey with peace and joy.

If at first we are hesitant to obey what we know we should, that is not the place we are destined to stay. We get to choose how we proceed.

What do you need to surrender today?

MEEKNESS

"Blessed are the meek, for they shall inherit the earth."
MATTHEW 5:5 ESV

God is not looking for extraordinary characters as His instruments, but He is looking for humble instruments through whom He can be honored throughout the ages. —A.B. Simpson, Days of Heaven Upon Earth

Meek is a word we don't often use in modern language. What does it mean? Meekness means humble and gentle, but it is also more than that. In submission to God, the meek trust in the one who guides them. They are humble, gentle, and surrendered.

God is our source of strength. When we yoke our hearts to him, we remain open to the source of all power, and we receive the strength we need. We rely on the Spirit to empower us by his presence. Let's not go it alone even for a day! When under the divine leadership of the Lord, we have all we ever need for every circumstance and season.

How meek are you? Pray for more humility, gentleness, and trust, and surrender your heart to God.

GROWING HUNGER

We know the love that God has for us, and we trust that love. God is love. Those who live in love live in God, and God lives in them.
1 JOHN 4:16 NCV

Let us occupy ourselves entirely in knowing God. The more we know Him, the more we will desire to know Him. As love increases with knowledge, the more we know God, the more we will truly love Him. We will learn to love Him equally in times of distress or in times of great joy. —Brother Lawrence, The Practice of the Presence of God

God's love is limitless. We have not, as a species, come close to scratching the surface of it. There is more power in his person than we have yet tasted. There is always more!

When we hunger and thirst for righteousness, we will be satisfied. Each new day, our hunger leads us to the righteous throne of our heavenly Father. We cannot reach the fullness of understanding. There are mysteries to uncover, and we will worship him in the awe and beauty of his glory as he uncovers more of his powerful love.

Let love lead you in prayer today.

CLOSER STILL

Draw near to God, and he will draw near to you.
JAMES 4:8 CSB

The great thing in prayer is to feel that we are putting our supplications into the bosom of omnipotent love.
—Andrew Murray, With Christ in the School of Prayer

When we draw near to God, we don't draw near to the edge of his throne room. We don't stand with backs against the wall and look on from a distance. As soon as we make a move toward the Lord, he makes a move toward us. He closes the distance.

There is nowhere we could go to escape the love of God. We couldn't outrun his presence. Where we are, he is already there. As soon as we turn our attention toward him, it's the instant we realize he is closer than we thought. Turn to your heavenly Father today, and receive what you need. More than what he offers, you get him. You get his attention, his presence, and his love. What abundance!

Draw near to God in prayer, and you will experience his nearness. Pray for greater awareness of his presence today.

FULLNESS

That you, being rooted and grounded in love, may be able to comprehend with all the saints what is the width and length and depth and height.

EPHESIANS 3:17-18 NKJV

Paul lived on his knees, that the Ephesian Church might measure the heights, breadths, and depths of an unmeasurable saintliness, and "be filled with all the fullness of God."
—E. M. Bounds, Power Through Prayer

Paul's prayer was not for his own satisfaction, but for the benefit and good of those he prayed for. He didn't just pray that the Ephesians would know a taste of God's love. He prayed that they would be able to comprehend the width, length, height and depth!

How often do we pray with that abundant spirit? Let's not pray for the meager thing—the lowest bar. Let's pray for the fullness just as Paul did. Christ's love is far larger than we have yet tasted. He wants more than a taste for us; he wants us to know his fullness.

When you pray for others, pray in the spirit of generosity and abundance.

KEEP KNOCKING

"I tell you, keep on asking, and you will receive what you ask for. Keep on seeking, and you will find. Keep on knocking, and the door will be opened to you."

LUKE 11:9 NLT

Seeming delays in God are no tokens of his displeasure; he may hide his face from his dearest saints. He loves to keep his people praying, and to find them ever knocking at the gate of heaven.
—John Bunyan, A Discourse Touching Prayer

Keep knocking on the door of heaven with your prayers. Oh, if only we lived in the fullness of God's presence with the light of his face as the sun that shines like the long summer days in the northern parts of the world. Where peace, love, joy, and hope reign without interruption, the glory of God's kingdom that we await so readily.

Until that blessed day, we wait, not with bated breath, but with active pursuit of the Lord. Keep on asking, and you will receive. Keep on seeking, and you will find. Keep on knocking, and the door will be opened. This is your invitation today and every day.

Pursue the Lord in prayer with passion today.

GLORIFYING THE TRINITY

"Go therefore and make disciples of all the nations, baptizing them in the name of the Father and of the Son and of the Holy Spirit."
MATTHEW 28:19 NKJV

Glorifying God has respect to all the persons in the Trinity; it respects God the Father who gave us life; God the Son, who lost his life for us; and God the Holy Ghost, who produces a new life in us; we must bring glory to the whole Trinity. —Thomas Watson, Divine Cordial

In prayer we can seek to glorify the Trinity—the Father, Son, and Holy Spirit. God the Father is our provider and the source of life. God the Son, gave up his throne and came to seek, serve, and save the lost. God the Holy Spirit is the one who works within us, bringing about transformation and new life.

How often do we include the Godhead in our prayers? May we be thoughtful in our prayers today, including each part of the Trinity and thanking God for who he is to us today and every day.

Pray to the Father in the name of the Son and in the power of the Spirit.

REFLECTIONS

Let us examine our ways and test them,
and let us return to the Lord.
Lamentations 3:40 NIV

Let me know myself, Lord, so that I may know You.
—St. Augustine, Soliloquies

We learn more about God as we discover what he put inside us. We don't want to spend so much time on inner reflection that we lose sight of who God is, who he has promised we are in him, and what he has for us in relationship to others. Still, self-reflection is an important part of prayer and connection.

Many of us get so used to doing what we're doing and thinking in ways we're accustomed to that we miss out on the growth potential of thoughtful reflection. No one is perfect. There is always room to grow in love, wisdom, and peace.

Reflect on your core beliefs about God and others, and see if there is any way that is out of step with how you behave. Pray for transformation in the grace of God.

AS YOU CAN

A poor widow came and put in two small copper coins, which make a penny. And he called his disciples to him and said to them, "Truly, I say to you, this poor widow has put in more than all those who are contributing to the offering box."

Mark 12:42-43 esv

When we cannot pray as we would, it is good to pray as we can.
—C. H. Spurgeon, Comfort for Those Whose Prayers Are Feeble

God does not expect us to offer more than we have. It is much better that we offer him the little we do have in surrender than make grand pledges with our imagined future resources. What matters is the here and now. What counts is what we have to offer today.

This is as true in prayer as in any other pursuit. The widow's mite didn't look like much to anyone from the outside, but it was a large percentage of what she had. God saw, and he knew. He knows when you only have the energy for a whispered prayer before sleep after a hard day. He honors what no one else sees. Trust him with your offering, no matter how insignificant it looks from the outside.

What do you have to offer God today?

COUNT IT JOY

My brothers and sisters, when you have many kinds of troubles, you should be full of joy, because you know that these troubles test your faith, and this will give you patience.

James 1:2-3 NCV

We do not always feel joyful, but we are always to count it joy.
—A.B. Simpson, Days of Heaven Upon Earth

What does it look like to count it all joy when the "it" includes suffering, pain, and hardship? Trouble does not mean we have done something wrong. Jesus had lots of trouble in his life—especially at the end of it—and he didn't do anything wrong in the sight of God. He did good: preaching truth, healing the sick, and offering compassion to those who didn't often receive it.

When we live in the light of God's love, that is our joy. Our joy is knowing him, following him, and becoming more like him. This doesn't free us from our troubles, but his present peace goes with us. When trials come, our joy remains deep and unwavering, for God's presence is unwavering in and for us.

Can you count your troubles as joy, knowing your Savior is with you in it?

PLEASING GOD

Since we know the fear of the Lord, we try to persuade people. What we are is plain to God, and I hope it is also plain to your consciences.

2 CORINTHIANS 5:11 CSB

Let us think often that our only business in this life is to please God. Perhaps all besides is but folly and vanity.
—Brother Lawrence, The Practice of the Presence of God

Our main priority shouldn't be to please the people around us. Should we not care about the effects of our words and actions? Of course! But we can't be living from a place of trying to pacify the expectations of those around us. We will never make everyone happy. That's not the goal. The goal is to live at peace, and that begins in us.

When pleasing God is our main priority, we come back to the foundation of his kingdom ways. The tenets of his law of love direct us in integrity, patience, wisdom, and truth. We don't have to throw our energy at a moving target or the expectations of others. We are the arrow, and God directs us in his steady hand.

Prayerfully consider whether you care more about what others think or what God thinks of you.

NO LIMITATIONS

Yes, again and again they tempted God,
And limited the Holy One of Israel.
Psalm 78:41 NKJV

Beware in your prayers, above everything else, of limiting God, not only by unbelief, but by fancying yourself that you know what He can do. —Andrew Murray, The Ministry of Intercession

What a shame it is when we limit our own expectations of God because of the fear of disappointment. Perhaps we live out of the past hurts we experienced, and we don't know how to risk trusting for better. But God is a God of abundance. He is doing a new thing in a new way, and we can trust his love-filled heart and gentle leadership in our lives.

We may think we know what God can do, but even our wildest imaginings are limited. Instead of trying to imagine what God can do, let's invite him into our prayers and expectations. Let's welcome his Holy Spirit's discernment, wisdom, and revelation to break open our limited understanding and hope for greater things.

Ask the Holy Spirit to reveal what God wants to do in the situations you cannot control.

EXPRESSIONS OF LIFE

"I give them eternal life, and they will never perish; and no one will snatch them out of My hand."

John 10:28 NASB

Prayer at its best is the expression of the total life.
—A. W. Tozer, The Root of Righteousness

As you draw near to God in prayer each day, your heart will need different things. You may find you're hungry for the wisdom of God's Word. You may be thirsty for the peace of his presence. You may have answers you are seeking, or find yourself resting in what is without feeling the rush to know what will be.

How does this find you today? What needs are present? What hunger wants to be filled in you? Take it all to the Lord in prayer, and trust that he will give you exactly what you need to quench your thirst. Consider the expression of life that you find in God's present nearness as you draw close to him.

When you are in Christ, you cannot be moved from him. Ask him to meet the thirst you have today with the living waters of his presence.

KNEES TO THE EARTH

How can they call on him to save them unless they believe in him? And how can they believe in him if they have never heard about him? And how can they hear about him unless someone tells them?
ROMANS 10:14 NLT

He that is never on his knees on earth, shall never stand upon his feet in heaven. —C. H. Spurgeon, Characteristics of Faith

The posture of kneeling before God in prayer is a physical representation of humbling ourselves before the King of creation. When we bow the knee, we honor God. Whether or not humbling yourself in this way is a regular practice, try it today. Kneel in prayer, and see how it affects the substance of your prayers.

Everything about life in God begins in prayer, in fellowship with him. We don't have to jump into the end goal for the day in order to begin where we must—before God in prayerful submission.

Let your body reflect the submission of your heart as you kneel before the Lord your God and maker.

UNFAILING LOVE

Love never fails. But whether there are prophecies, they will fail; whether there are tongues, they will cease; whether there is knowledge, it will vanish away.

1 CORINTHIANS 13:8 NKJV

In heaven we will need no repentance, because we will have no sin. We will not need faith, because we will see God face to face. But love to God will abide forever. Love never fails.
—Thomas Watson, The Ten Commandments

Love never ends. While many of our earthly experiences will cease—fighting, language barriers, confusion, and isolation—the nature of God's kingdom will last forever. Why not live with those eternal values as our priorities now?

When we stray from love, peace, hope, and grace, let's welcome God to realign our hearts, as we realign our actions. We get to choose better each day. One day—in the eternal realm of his kingdom—we will not need to actively choose a better way. There will be ease in doing what is right, for there will be no sin to repent from or weakness to keep us from walking in his light. But, for now, we lean on his grace to refine us.

Pray for the power of God's love to empower you to choose better today.

PRAY FOR WORKERS

"The harvest is plentiful but the workers are few. Ask the Lord of the harvest, therefore, to send out workers into his harvest field."
Matthew 9:37-38 niv

When we calmly reflect upon the fact that the progress of our Lord's Kingdom is dependent upon prayer, it is sad to think that we give so little time to the holy exercise. —E. M. Bounds, Purpose in Prayer

Jesus did not tell his followers, "Pray that the work will get done." He said, "Ask for the Lord to send out workers into the field." How often do we disconnect the work or the need from the hands that can meet it?

When you see a need today, don't just pray that the need will get met, pray for the people who can directly meet that need. Pray that their hearts would be moved to partner with the Lord. Pray for hands to serve, minds to comprehend, and hearts to receive. God delights in partnering with people; it's how he designed things from the beginning. Let's pray for people to be moved!

Pray for the workers to meet the needs in the world.

HOPEFUL WAITING

We will wait for the Lord.
He helps us and protects us.
Psalm 33:20 esv

We are in such a habit of evaluating God and His work in us by what we feel that it is very likely that on some occasions we will be discouraged because we do not feel any special blessing. Above everything, when you wait on God, you must do so in the spirit of hope.
—Andrew Murray, Waiting on God

It takes thoughtfulness to remain in a state of hopeful waiting. Especially when we find the time draws long. When discouragement begins to set in, let's ask for the Spirit of hope to breathe on us.

The Spirit's wind is like opening the windows on a spring day after a long winter. Fresh air clears the mustiness out of the home. When we open the windows of our heart to the Lord, welcoming him through the open door, he comes in and sets to freshening our inner world. His wind blows off the cobwebs of discouragement. His presence brings the light of peace to darkened corners. Hopeful waiting is a practice, and we can open our hearts to the refreshing presence of God any time.

Pray and invite the Holy Spirit to refresh your heart and expectations.

FOUNDATIONS OF FAITH

The God of all grace, who called you to his eternal glory in Christ, will himself restore, establish, strengthen, and support you after you have suffered a little while.

1 Peter 5:10 CSB

God is ever wanting to add to us, to develop us, to enlarge us, to teach us more and more, but it is ever in the line of things which He has already taught us, and in which we have been established.
—A.B. Simpson, Days of Heaven Upon Earth

God is able to restore what seems completely destroyed. If we struggle to hope, let's remember that it is the perfect place to invite God's redemptive love to shine. We cannot avoid suffering in this life, but we don't have to live in despair. Though much may have been stripped, the foundation remains sure in him.

While there is always more to experience, it does not void the foundation of faith our lives are built upon. We have been established by grace, and that will always be true. As the testing of this life brings opportunities to grow, let's not leave behind the foundation.

Ask God to remind you of the foundations of your faith.

GO TO GOD

Those who go to God Most High for safety
will be protected by the Almighty.
Psalm 91:1 NCV

When you rise in the morning, your business so urgent, that with a hurried word or two of prayer, out you go into the world; and at night, worn out and tired, you give God the meager leftovers of the day, the consequence is that you have no communion with Him. The reason we do not have more true Christianity among us now is because we do not have more secret prayer.
—C. H. Spurgeon, Prayer and Spiritual Warfare

Communion with God is cultivated. It is not a mere hello that you might offer an acquaintance. The more you go to him, the more deeply you get to know him. You become accustomed to sharing the deepest parts of your heart and life with him, and he becomes to you like a wise counselor and faithful friend.

The more time you spend with God, listening to his heart, reading his Word, and getting to know his character, the more you will want to go to him.

Turn to the Lord throughout your day and invite him to reveal himself to you in deeper ways.

HIDDEN DESIRES

Delight yourself in the Lord;
And He will give you the desires of your heart.
Psalm 37:4 NASB

There is another inward kind of prayer without ceasing, which is the desire of the heart. Whatever else you are doing, if you do but long for that Sabbath, you do not cease to pray. If you would never cease to pray, never cease to long after it. The continuance of thy longing is the continuance of thy prayer.
—St. Augustine, Expositions on the Book of Psalms

God knows the truest desires of your heart. That dream you haven't talked about in a while? He sees it. That longing you've stopped saying out loud? He knows. Continue to pursue the Lord, and he will give you the desires of your heart. Delight yourself in him, and find your peace and joy in his presence. Trust him with the rest.

The longing of the not yet keeps us tethered to eternity. There is a fullness of satisfaction that is coming in the power of God's love in his eternal kingdom. You can trust him to meet you while you wait.

Ask God to meet you in your longings.

SPIRIT POWER

You, dear friends, must build each other up in your most holy faith, pray in the power of the Holy Spirit.
JUDE 1:20 NLT

The Christian doctrine of prayer is that it is the believer's privilege to be taught by the Spirit of God Himself to know what the will of God is and not to ask for the things that our foolishness would prompt us to ask for but to ask for things that the never-erring Spirit of God prompts us to ask for. True prayer is prayer "in the Spirit," that is, the prayer which the Spirit inspires and directs. —R. A. Torrey, How to Pray

Prayer does not end with us. It begins with us turning our hearts and attention to the Lord. It requires calling out—whether with a whisper, a cry, or a shout—as we reach out to God. But this is not all. It is our powerful privilege to be taught by the Spirit of God to know what to pray, how to pray, and how to proceed.

As we bend our will to the Lord's, the Spirit gives insight into the heart of God and provides powerful partnership as we let his scalpel go directly to what needs to be addressed, with precision and power.

Lean on the Holy Spirit to direct your prayers.

WHISPERED HALLELUJAHS

The sacrifice of the wicked is an abomination to the Lord,
But the prayer of the upright is His delight.
Proverbs 15:8 NKJV

Lift up your heart to Him during your meals and in company; the least little remembrance will always be the most pleasing to Him. One need not cry out very loudly; He is nearer to us than we think.
—Brother Lawrence, The Practice of the Presence of God

God is not impressed by loud, ornate prayers. He isn't moved by perfectly crafted language. If the words are beautiful but shallow, what does any of it matter? Better to stumble over our words and have a heart that is truly seeking him than to sound smart but be full of pride.

God is close to the humble and lifts up those who have been defeated. He is with the vulnerable and beaten down. He is looking for people who turn their minds to him and who open their hearts to him. Turn your attention to Jesus, ask him to guide you as you pray, and invite him to meet you. Whisper hallelujah when you see his love in the world, and when you sense his nearness.

Give God little acknowledgments throughout your day.

Ever-Living Intercessor

It is Christ who died, and furthermore is also risen, who is even at the right hand of God, who also makes intercession for us.

Romans 8:34 NKJV

Christ teaches us to pray not only by example, by instruction, by command, by promises, but by showing us himself, the ever-living Intercessor, as our Life. It is when we believe this, and go and abide in Him for our prayer-life too, that our fears of not being able to pray aright will vanish, and we shall joyfully and triumphantly trust our Lord to teach us to pray, to be Himself the life and the power of our prayer.
—Andrew Murray, With Christ in the School of Prayer

Jesus Christ is not only our Savior, but he is also our intercessor. He pleads our case before the Father, bringing us into his own loving heart. Jesus is praying for you. How does that make you feel? Does it stir your heart with gratitude? Does it seem too good to be true?

If you notice feelings of shame, like it's too much for the Savior to be praying for you specifically, bring that to him. Ask him to shine his light on your heart, over your mind, and break the yoke of shame.

Depend on Jesus' powerful work as your intercessor.

WITHOUT HINDRANCE

He proclaimed the kingdom of God and taught about the Lord Jesus Christ—with all boldness and without hindrance!
ACTS 28:31 NIV

Contemporaries relate that hearing Martin Luther pray was "an experience in theology". They said the reformer began praying with such humility that he could be pitied, only to proceed with such boldness before God that the human hearer would fear for him.
—Roland Bainton, Here I Stand

God invites our boldest prayers. We don't have to shrink in his presence. If we have surrendered our lives to him and follow his ways, what should keep us from praying with confidence? Hebrews 4:16 reminds us that we should approach God's throne of grace with confidence.

If people heard you praying, what would they think? Would they wonder if you're fearful of him? Maybe your casual tone would give the impression that you're talking to someone you know well. Step outside of yourself and imagine what you would think if your overheard your private prayers.

Pray to God from a place of confidence in his love for you.

CLEANSED AND FREE

If we confess our sins, he is faithful and just to forgive us our sins and to cleanse us from all unrighteousness.
1 JOHN 1:9 ESV

No, not despairingly come I to Thee. No, not distrustingly, bend I the knee. Sin hath gone over me, yet is this still my plea. Jesus hath died. Ah, mine iniquity crimson has been, infinite, infinite. Sin upon sin: sin of not loving Thee, sin of not trusting Thee. Infinite sin. Lord, I confess to thee sadly my sin. All I am, tell I Thee, all I have been. Purge Thou my sin away. Wash Thou my soul this day. Lord, make me clean! —D. L. Moody, Prevailing Prayer

Moody's prayer reflects a heart that wants to be clean before the Lord. It interweaves Scripture with the power of Christ's sacrifice, and it offers surrender in the place of weakness. Oh, that we would be clean before God. And Jesus Christ has made that possible!

Whenever we are convicted of sin, we should pray for forgiveness and change our ways. The changing is what we do as cleansed, liberated, and loved children of God. We cannot change the direction of our actions until we confess that we have erred. Let's repent and let the power of God's love transform our hearts and minds.

Ask God to cleanse your heart completely.

THE ONLY SAVIOR

"Jesus is the only One who can save people. No one else in the world is able to save us."
ACTS 4:12 NCV

Three wishes Paul had, and they were all about Christ; that he might be found in Christ, be with Christ, and magnify Christ.
—Thomas Watson, Divine Cordial

Paul's life was completely changed by a dramatic encounter with the Lord. He had been persecuting the disciples and followers of Jesus as a Pharisee. He did not only make their lives difficult; he put some to death. And yet it was Jesus who stopped him on the road to Damascus as he traveled, blinding him with light and inviting Saul to follow him. He gave him a new name, and offered him a new path.

From there, Paul became an apostle. He followed passionately after God, giving up his previous life of prestige and humbling himself with the other disciples. In the end, it was Christ the Savior Paul sought, proclaimed, and lived for. Christ was the highest aim.

Paul changed his ways, and so can you. Pray for the power of God to meet you and direct you.

WHATEVER WE ASK

If we know that he hears whatever we ask, we know that we have what we have asked of him.

1 John 5:15 CSB

When the Creator gives His creature the power of thirst, it is because water exists to meet its thirst. When He creates hunger, there is food to correspond to the appetite. Even so, when He inclines men to pray, it is because prayer has a corresponding blessing connected with it.
—C. H. Spurgeon, Prayer Certified of Success

If you have a longing in your heart—a thirst or hunger inside of you—it is because God put it there. You don't have to be shy when you come to God with the reflection of that request. He delights in meeting your needs and satisfying your thirst.

When you feel inclined to ask God for something, think about whether what you're asking is based in mirroring someone else's experience or because you actually want it. Children ask their parents for things all the time, and not every ask reflects true desire. Bring God your longings, and ask him to meet you in them.

Reflect on the things you actually have spiritual and soul hunger for today, and ask for those things.

AT WORK IN THE DETAILS

We know that God causes all things to work together for good to those who love God, to those who are called according to His purpose.
Romans 8:28 NASB

The difficulties of life do not have to be unbearable. It is the way we look at them—through faith or unbelief—that makes them seem so. We must be convinced that our Father is full of love for us and that He only permits trials to come our way for our own good.
—Brother Lawrence, The Practice of the Presence of God

Our perspective of God largely shapes the way we pray. If we let challenges dictate whether God is good or not, we will struggle to know his peace in the midst of them.

God is at work in the details of our lives. He causes all things to work together for good. Does that mean all things will feel good? By no means! You can be assured that with every breath you are breathing, his gracious redemption is working through the details of your story. You may not see the goodness yet, but hold on. Keep trusting, for the one who started a good work in you will carry it on to completion until Christ returns (Philippians 1:6). That's a Scripture promise you can hold on to!

Ask God to show you how he is moving in the details of your life.

THANK JESUS

Whatever you do or say, do it as a representative of the Lord Jesus, giving thanks through him to God the Father.
Colossians 3:17 NLT

Patient, persevering, believing prayer that is offered up to God in the name of the Lord Jesus has always brought the blessing sooner or later. —Andrew Murray, With Christ in the School of Prayer

As we continually thank Jesus for what he does for, in, and through us, we give him honor. In the waiting, when endurance and perseverance are required, a thankful heart keeps us connected to his goodness. Where there is heaviness, there is also peace. Where there is darkness, there is also light. Where there is pain, there is also joy.

Can you give God thanks in the areas he is requiring you to be patient? Don't give up on him or on your journey. He knows what he is doing, and he has not lost the plot or gotten distracted. He is doing what needs to be done, setting the pieces in place, to bring restoration and hope.

The blessing in answer to your prayer is coming. Thank him in the meantime.

BY FAITH

It is of faith that it might be according to grace, so that the promise might be sure to all the seed, not only to those who are of the law, but also to those who are of the faith of Abraham, who is the father of us all.

Romans 4:16 NKJV

Forgiveness, cleansing, regeneration, the Holy Spirit, all answers to prayer, are given to faith and received by faith. There is no other way. This is common evangelical doctrine and is accepted wherever the cross of Christ is understood. —A.W. Tozer, The Root of Righteousness

By faith we are saved, and by faith we receive the answers to our prayers. Faith is the spark that catches the kindling and sets the fire of our hearts ablaze. It does not need to be a fully formed fire already!

Where have you underplayed the role that faith has played in your life? Where have you kept yourself from seeing the power of it in the little sparks around you? Faith can be as tiny as a mustard seed and make a mountain move from its place. Let the little sparks of faith move you in surrender today.

Follow the sparks. God is putting them in your life for a reason.

POWER OF HOLINESS

Make every effort to live in peace with everyone and to be holy; without holiness no one will see the Lord.
Hebrews 12:14 NIV

A prayerless age will have but scant models of divine power. The age may be a better age than the past, but there is an infinite distance between the betterment of an age by the force of an advancing civilization and its betterment by the increase of holiness and Christlikeness by the energy of prayer.
—E. M. Bounds, Power Through Prayer

If we want to know the power of prayer and God's miraculous move in our lives, communities, nations, and the world, we have to know what it is to be holy as God is holy. According to First Peter, this means being obedient to God's ways and refusing to conform to the ways of this world.

Jesus Christ purifies us from sin and makes us new in his grace, but our willingness to walk in his ways and humble ourselves is what makes us holy. As we walk in integrity, refuse to let corruption infiltrate our lives, and quickly respond to God's correction, we live in the power of holiness.

Ask the Spirit to help make you holy, humble, and quick to respond.

ASK FOR WISDOM

If any of you lacks wisdom, let him ask God, who gives generously to all without reproach, and it will be given him.

JAMES 1:5 ESV

A godly man is on the mount of prayer every day. He begins the day with prayer. Before he opens his shop, he opens his heart to God! We burn sweet incense in our houses; a godly man's house is "a house of incense"; he airs it with the incense of prayer. He engages in no business without seeking God. A godly man consults God in everything; he asks God's permission and his blessing.
—Thomas Watson, The Godly Man's Picture

Wisdom is not the same thing as being knowledgeable. Knowing information but not knowing how to apply it is useless. Wisdom is practical. It is clear. It is filled with the fruit of the Spirit. Do you want more wisdom? Read the Proverbs. Ask the Spirit to teach you.

Learn from those who are temperate, grounded, slow to anger, and offer words of advice only when asked. Learn from people who are patient, gentle, and known for their honesty. Pattern your life after Jesus—wisdom personified—and you cannot go wrong.

Seek God for wisdom, and when you see it in others, honor it.

WHAT GOD WANTS

Teach me to do what you want,
because you are my God.
Let your good Spirit
lead me on level ground.
Psalm 143:10 NCV

Give, O Lord, what Thou commandest, and then command what Thou wilt. —St. Augustine, Confessions

When you pray, do you think more of what you want or what God wants? Some days may vary, but if most of our prayers have more to do with what we want and we don't spend a lot of time asking for what God wants (or at least the revelation of it), we miss out on what walking with God in humble submission can be like.

God wants us to know him. He wants us to discover how easy to please he is (Matthew 11:29), how much he cares for us (1 Peter 5:7), and how freely he gives us his strength and peace (Psalm 29:11). But if you notice, those things all have to do with us too, right? The very nature of relationship is how we connect to each other. Today, begin in the place of asking God to reveal what he wants.

Spend time in prayer asking God to teach you what he wants, and follow his wisdom with your actions.

RESISTANCE

Submit to God. Resist the devil, and he will flee from you.
James 4:7 CSB

Do not be discouraged by the resistance you will encounter from your human nature; you must go against your human inclinations. Often, in the beginning, you will think that you are wasting time, but you must go on, be determined and persevere in it until death, despite all the difficulties. —Brother Lawrence, The Practice of the Presence of God

When we submit our hearts to God, we allow him first place. His voice, his ways, his nature have more authority than anything else. It is a practice to submit ourselves to God each day. It won't happen by accident. As we yield our will to the Lord's and ask him to guide us, he goes with us and provides grace to strengthen us.

Just because we feel resistance—either inside of us, from others, or from society—does not mean that we are destined to give into that resistance. We get to choose what we do in that moment. Will we resist the urge to do the easy thing when it's not the right thing? Resist, and that urge will flee.

Prayer keeps us submitted to God. Pray when you need grace to resist temptation.

HEAVEN'S MYSTERIES

He is the image of the invisible God, the firstborn of all creation: for by Him all things were created, both in the heavens and on earth, visible and invisible, whether thrones, or dominions, or rulers, or authorities—all things have been created through Him and for Him.

COLOSSIANS 1:15-16 NASB

We must begin to believe that God, in the mystery of prayer, has entrusted us with a force that can move the Heavenly world, and can bring its power down to earth.
—Andrew Murray, The Ministry of Intercession

All things were created through Christ and for him. He is the image of the invisible God! What heavenly mysteries he revealed through his nature, his ministry, his miracles, and submission. Let's not ignore the power of Christ's humility in the face of power-hungry people. He did not fight dirty. He stayed true to the nature of the Father, and leaned on his power to walk in the truth.

If we want to know the power of God through our prayer lives, let's join our hearts to the mystery of Christ. We can partner with God's heavenly authority and pray as Jesus taught us, "on earth as it is in heaven."

Powerful prayer begins in Christ. Pray for his power to move in and through you.

THE MIND OF CHRIST

Think about the things of heaven, not the things of earth.
COLOSSIANS 3:2 NLT

The best way to control our thoughts is to offer the mind to God in complete surrender. The Holy Spirit will accept it and take control of it immediately. Then it will be relatively easy to think on spiritual things, especially if we train our thought by long periods of daily prayer. Long practice in the art of mental prayer (that is, talking to God inwardly as we work or [relax]) will help to form the habit of holy thought. —A.W. Tozer, Of God and Men

How often do you offer God the screen of your mind? In prayer today, offer God what is in you—the cares, the thoughts, the burdens, and the sparks of inspiration—and when you've done that, invite the Spirit into your mind with complete surrender.

The Spirit brings light, life, and clarity. The Spirit brings peace to the chaos. The Spirit brings hope to desolation. It is much easier to yield to the Spirit's work than to strive to do it ourselves. Surrender opens the door, removes our inner resistance, and welcomes the Spirit of love to do God's work.

Surrender your mind to the Spirit, and notice how your perspective shifts throughout the day.

GIVE EAR

Give ear to my words, O Lord,
Consider my meditation.
Give heed to the voice of my cry,
My King and my God,
For to You I will pray.
Psalm 5:1-2 NKJV

We must remember that the goal of prayer is the ear of God. Unless that is gained the prayer has utterly failed.
—E. M. Bounds, Purpose in Prayer

Prayer is not about showing off to others. It's not about gaining approval from those we pray with. Prayer is always about connecting with God. It is his ear that we whisper into. It is his heart that we deposit our prayers into.

If prayer feels like a practice you do because you should, ask God to meet you in it today. Speak directly to his listening ear. Then, as a reciprocal practice, listen for what he has to say to you. Direct your words to him, and then open the ears of your heart to listen for what he wants to speak to you.

God loves to show us what he's like. In prayer, he listens. Take his example and do the same.

RECOGNIZABLE FRUIT

"By their fruit you will recognize them. Do people pick grapes from thornbushes, or figs from thistles?"
Matthew 7:16 NIV

The tree of the promise will not drop its fruit unless shaken by the hand of prayer. —Thomas Watson, The Ten Commandments

Jesus said that it is by the fruit of our lives that we can recognize what kind of tree we are. In the same way, the prayers we pray bring evidence of how persistent we are to know God through fellowship and partnering with him.

The fruit of the Spirit is as follows: love, joy, peace, forbearance, kindness, goodness, faithfulness, gentleness and self-control. There is no law against these attributes (Galatians 5:22-23). When we live by the Spirit, we keep in step with the Spirit, and we do this through prayer, partnership, and obedience. If we want good fruit—the fruit of God's kingdom—to fill our lives, then we have to be submitted to God.

Pray for God to show you where you could partner more with his fruit-bearing power.

FOUNTAIN OF LIFE

If Christ is in you, although the body is dead because of sin, the Spirit is life because of righteousness.
ROMANS 8:10 ESV

There is nothing so delightful as this consciousness of the very life and heart of Christ within us, the trust that springs spontaneously within our breast, the prayer that prays itself, and the song that sings its joyous triumph even when all around is dark and strange.
—A.W. Tozer, The Pursuit of God

There are seasons of life when we are filled with all that we need, and the gifts of God's grace overflow us with gratitude, joy, and peace. We cannot give from an empty cup. In the same way, we cannot hold back the life that overflows from a cup spilling over.

If Christ is in you, the Spirit of life resides in your being. You have access to the very source of love, peace, joy, hope, and grace. There is nothing you need for your soul that he does not supply. Let's drink from the fountain of life.

Ask the Lord to spring up within you and bring refreshing that overflows.

LIVE IN HIS PRESENCE

Happy are the people who live at your Temple;
they are always praising you.
PSALM 84:3 NCV

O, let the place of secret prayer become to me the most beloved spot on earth. —Andrew Murray, With Christ in the School of Prayer

There is an open invitation for all who come to the Lord to live in his presence. We can stay there because we have become temples of God. We don't have to sell our homes and take up residence in a sacred space. Wherever we are is sacred.

How could this perspective change the way you pray? You can always praise God, letting the light of his love shine on your heart. You are never without him, and that means you are never without a reason to praise! Live in the awareness of his presence in you, and you will have every reason to reach out to him in joy.

Thank God for the power of his presence with you in this moment.

KEEP ASKING

"You will seek me and find me
when you search for me with all your heart."
JEREMIAH 29:13 CSB

If God's mercies were to come to us unasked, they would not be half as useful as they now are, when they have to be sought for.
—C. H. Spurgeon, Order and Argument in Prayer

Have you ever walked into a room packed with stuff? Though there may be useful things hidden in the abundance, it can be difficult to know what's there. Though it might seem like there is everything needed in that room, what use is it if it isn't accessible?

When we feel our need, prayer sends us to the source. God is able to go into a crowded room and pick out exactly what is needed at the right time. Trust the Spirit to bring you what you need. Search for the Lord rather than the gifts he has to offer. You will get those too, surely, but he is the one worth knowing.

Ask the Lord for help in mundane things and notice what happens.

ACCEPT IT

"Whatever you ask in prayer, believing, you will receive it all."
MATTHEW 21:22 NASB

Faith is not hope, not a mere expectation of future things, but a present receiving of that which is promised in a real and substantial way. It is accepting, not expecting. —A.B. Simpson, Standing on Faith

Hope and faith are often confused. Hope looks ahead with the knowledge that there is breakthrough, goodness, peace, and the faithfulness of God coming. Faith receives the promises of God in the present, and it acts as if they are already guaranteed.

Do you pray more from a place of hope or faith? Do you live from a place of hopeful expectation of good things to come, or do you live like Noah or Abraham, building for what's coming? Both belong. They are partners in our prayer lives. Let's ask God for more faith that moves us in action today and the peace of trust that remains present as we hope.

Pray for both the fruit of hope and faith to be evident in your heart and life.

PLANS FOR GOOD

"For I know the plans I have for you," says the Lord.
"They are plans for good and not for disaster,
to give you a future and a hope."
Jeremiah 29:11 NLT

That all things are possible to him who believes, that they are less difficult to him who hopes, they are more easy to him who loves, and still more easy to him who perseveres in the practice of these three virtues.
—Brother Lawrence, The Practice of the Presence of God

Faith, hope, and love. These are the things Scripture says will last into eternity. Faith and hope are not only something we experience in this life, and we should put them into practice each day. As for love: God is love. Those who love are born of God.

The plans of God are full of goodness. They are to offer hope, faith, and love with each step. When we trust the heart of God, it is easier to follow in the ways of God. Everything is possible for the one who puts their hope in God, follows it up with actions of faith, and lets everything that goes against love fall away.

Which of these virtues do you need more of today: faith, hope, or love?

PRAYERFUL REPENTANCE

"I dwell in the high and holy place,
With him who has a contrite and humble spirit,
To revive the spirit of the humble,
And to revive the heart of the contrite ones."
Isaiah 57:15 NKJV

Prayer for revival will prevail when it is accompanied by radical amendment of life, not before. All-night prayer meetings that are not preceded by practical repentance may actually be displeasing to God. "To obey is better than sacrifice." We must return to New Testament Christianity, not in creed only but in complete manner of life as well.
—A. W. Tozer, The Root of Righteousness

Revival begins in the heart. It doesn't happen overnight. It is a powerful revelation of the devotion of God's people in prayer. Revival is fought for in the hearts of God's people. It isn't a chance encounter!

We must humble our hearts before God. This is where it starts. Humbling ourselves, we become convicted of the error of our ways by the power of the Spirit; there is no shame in this conviction. There is clarity, and a ready repentance. Practical repentance and prayerful devotion go together to ready the heart for revival.

Humble yourself before God, and ask him to highlight anything in you that requires repentance.

THE POWER OF INTEGRITY

"I the LORD search the heart
and examine the mind,
to reward each person according to their conduct,
according to what their deeds deserve."
JEREMIAH 17:10 NIV

The Church is looking for better methods; God is looking for better men.
—E. M. Bounds, Power Through Prayer

We cannot outsmart God. He is not impressed by innovations or forward thinking. He does not care about the outer trappings. He looks at the heart. He's looking for people of integrity, people who are willing to be humble, admit when they're wrong, and choose love above everything else.

Loving action is expressed in many ways. It is revealed through generosity toward the poor, Kindness toward neighbors, and welcoming the immigrant. It is shown by encouraging one another with our words and offering acts of support. When we remain open to instruction and direction, nothing God says will offend us.

Where does your substance lie? Let your answer direct your prayers.

POTENT PRAYERS

"Beware of practicing your righteousness before other people in order to be seen by them, for then you will have no reward from your Father who is in heaven."

Matthew 6:1 esv

He who neglects to pray alone and in private, however assiduously he frequents public meetings, there gives his prayers to the wind.
—John Calvin, Institutes of the Christian Religion

If we want to have a powerful prayer life, it begins in our personal prayer time. The more we cultivate relationship with the Lord, the more we will know him. The more we know him, the more prepared we are to partner with him in public.

If we only pray when others can hear us, what's the point? Who are we trying to prove ourselves to? God is the one who listens and responds. He can do that as readily in the quiet, secret place. Let's prioritize prayer when we're alone. God reveals himself to those who earnestly seek him. If we don't do that in our own time, then it isn't earnest at all.

Be sure to connect with God when no one else can see.

OBEY GOD

Peter and the other apostles answered, "We must obey God, not human authority!"
Acts 5:29 NCV

Obedience without fervency is like a sacrifice without fire. Why should our obedience not be lively and fervent? God deserves the flower and strength of our affections. —Thomas Watson, The Ten Commandments

Prayer isn't a suggestion. It's a lifeline. It is where we unburden our hearts and receive God's peace. It is how we open our hearts to the Spirit and welcome his wisdom. Listening prayer is an attitude of sitting before the Lord, waiting to hear his voice. Why does God want us to pray, to talk to him and listen for his voice? It is how we fellowship with him, how we enter beyond the veil and receive all we need to live a godly life.

Obedience becomes much easier when we know the heart of the one who calls us. He is kind even in correction. He is just and merciful. He is full of peace and hope, wisdom and joy. There is nothing good that originated outside of him.

When you hesitate to press into prayer, remember the beauty of the one you turn toward.

CONTENTED

Godliness with contentment is great gain. For we brought nothing into the world, and we can take nothing out. If we have food and clothing, we will be content with these.

1 Timothy 6:6-8 CSB

Whoever possesses the present moment possesses God; whoever possesses the present moment possesses everything. The present moment is enough don't let anything trouble you.
—St. Teresa of Ávila, The Life of Teresa of Jesus

Contentment isn't possible in any moment but the present. We can't build it up for tomorrow or take it with us from yesterday. It is born, cultivated, and embraced here and now. Godliness with contentment is great gain. We need open channels of gratitude and prayer to keep coming back to a place of peace.

We cannot control what happened yesterday, and we cannot predict what tomorrow will bring. It's not our job to know! We are to rest in the power of God's faithfulness. We are to trust his sufficient grace as we receive it.

Take this very moment to connect with God in gratitude.

WHOLEHEARTED SURRENDER

"'You shall love the Lord your God with all your heart, and with all your soul, and with all your mind.'"
MATTHEW 22:37 NASB

We might be wise to follow the insight of the enraptured heart rather than the more cautious reasoning of the theological mind.
—A. W. Tozer, The Knowledge of the Holy

Knowledge is no substitute for relationship. We can learn about God and miss out on what it is to really know him in fellowship. Prayer takes us from what we know to wholehearted connection. It opens the pathway from our heart to the Lord's. It is the place where God meets us, transforming us from the inside out.

Love is not something we only do in our hearts. It is not something we only choose in our minds. It is not only the actions we live out in relation to others. It is all of these and more. The expression of love is something that happens with our entire being. We are wholly loved, and we get to wholly love God in return.

Ask God to move your love from your head to your heart.

HAND IN HAND

Never be lazy, but work hard and serve the Lord enthusiastically.
ROMANS 12:11 NLT

After praying, Elisha implemented the actions. Prayer and action must go together. Action without prayer: presumption. Prayer without action: hypocrisy. —C. H. Spurgeon, The Soul Winner

Whatever we start in prayer doesn't end there. We move from that place with surrender and concerted effort. If our actions don't partner with our prayers, what are we even doing? Action without prayer is presumption. And prayer without action is hypocrisy.

Hypocrisy may seem like a harsh way to put it, but it is fitting. Hypocrisy means claiming to have one set of standards or beliefs but acting against them. If we say we trust God in our prayers and then live recklessly, God will remain faithful, but our own lives will be exposed for the dissonance. Prayer and action go together. Follow up your trust with a yielded heart that does the good it knows to do.

Ask God to show you how you can live with prayerful action.

GRACE AND SUPPLICATION

"I will pour on the house of David and on the inhabitants of Jerusalem the Spirit of grace and supplication; then they will look on Me whom they pierced. Yes, they will mourn for Him as one mourns for his only son, and grieve for Him as one grieves for a firstborn."

ZECHARIAH 12:10 NKJV

The secret of all true and effective praying is knowing the Holy Spirit as "the Spirit of grace and of supplication."
—R.A Torrey, The Person and Work of the Holy Spirit

Supplication is a type of prayer. It is most often translated as meaning "to plead humbly." We know that God is full of grace. He meets us in our weakness, offering us strength. The Spirit of grace and supplication moves on our hearts in prayer to bring us humbly before the throne of grace to receive all that we need.

Humble yourself before the Lord, and he will lift you up. Ask him for what you need, not from a place of desperation or pride, but from authentic connection. It might take you some time in your prayer time to get there, and that's okay. Humble your heart first, and the rest will come.

Plead humbly before your God today.

BUILT ON THE ROCK

"I tell you that you are Peter, and on this rock I will build my church, and the gates of Hades will not overcome it."

MATTHEW 16:18 NIV

The true Church of Jesus Christ will never be overwhelmed by the world. The waters may swirl around us, but the Lord has promised to build His Church and keep it strong until He returns.
—A.B. Simpson, The Life of Prayer

God has not given up on humanity. No matter how awful things seem in the moment, his heart moves in love toward the people he has made. There is not a time in history when the church has disappeared, and that won't happen now either. Though the waters swirl around us, the people of God will not be moved from his foundation of mercy.

It is easy to look around at the chaos in the world and feel discouraged. Take it to the Lord in prayer! Pray for the things that burden your heart. Pray for the people who are hurting, and the people you see hurting them. Stay tethered to the anchor of hope in Christ's presence. He is still near, still working, and he will continue.

Pray for the Church to stand strong in the love of Christ.

MAJESTIC MEDITATIONS

On the glorious splendor of your majesty,
and on your wondrous works, I will meditate.
PSALM 145:5 ESV

We should feed and nourish our souls with high notions of God; which would yield us great joy in being devoted to Him.
—Brother Lawrence, The Practice of the Presence of God

What we spend time thinking about are the things on which we meditate. This is a good reminder to take stock of our thoughts. What are the things we most often mull over? If what you find is not what you'd hoped it would be, it's not too late to change the script. Turn your attention to God. It can shift your perspective completely.

Instead of overthinking that hard interaction you had earlier, what if you turned your attention to the God who made the starry skies? Get out into nature if it helps you. You are a tiny part of this large world. Look at the wonderful things around you. They are small reflections of God's great glory. You are a tiny reflection of God's goodness. If all this majesty is but a glimpse, how glorious our God truly is, and how worthy of praise.

Use prayerful meditation as a perspective shift today.

THE ABUNDANT LIFE

"A thief comes to steal and kill and destroy, but I came to give life—life in all its fullness."

JOHN 10:10 NCV

Prayer is the pulse of the spiritual life. It is the great means by which ministers and laypeople alike receive the blessing and power of heaven. Persevering and believing prayer precludes a strong and abundant life. —Andrew Murray, The Prayer Life

If we want to take stock of our spiritual lives, prayer is a good place to look. As Murray put it, "Prayer is the pulse of the spiritual life." Even if we have the faintest heartbeat, prayer infuses our spiritual hearts with fervor. It is where the power and blessings flow.

If we want to have a strong spiritual life, we cannot ignore the importance of prayer. If we want to live in the abundance of God's kingdom, we cannot work ourselves there. We have to prioritize our prayer lives. Everything else flows from the heart, and so does the power of prayer!

Jesus offers you the fullness of his life. Spend time in prayer seeking after him today.

PREPARE YOUR HEART

LORD, you have heard the desire of the humble;
you will strengthen their hearts.
You will listen carefully.
PSALM 10:17 CSB

A prepared heart is much better than a prepared sermon. A prepared heart will make a prepared sermon.
—E. M. Bounds, Power Through Prayer

In order to prepare our hearts, we humble ourselves before the Lord. There really is no other way. It is good to ready ourselves for the work we need to do, but prayer is how we connect to the Spirit of God. With a heart that is open to the leadership of the Lord, we remain ready to hear and move.

Jesus told his disciples in Mark 13:11, "Don't worry beforehand what you will say, but say whatever is given to you at that time, for it isn't you speaking, but the Holy Spirit." You can rely on the Spirit to give you the right words at the right time. Spend a little less time on the specifics of what you will say and more time connecting to God.

Prioritize more time in prayer, and trust God with the rest.

MEDIATOR

Since we have a great high priest who has passed through the heavens, Jesus the Son of God, let's hold firmly to our confession.
HEBREWS 4:14 NASB

God cannot be really invoked by us and his name glorified, except through Christ the mediator; for it is he alone who sanctifies our lips, which otherwise are unclean, to sing the praises of God; and it is he who opens a way for our prayers, who in short performs the office of a priest, presenting himself before God in our name.
—John Calvin, Commentary on Hebrews

Jesus Christ is our mediator before the Father. Everything goes through him. This is very good news for us! He is our gracious Savior and powerful Redeemer. He is the one who knows us well. He understands the limits of humanity, having lived in this world. He has compassion for us in ways we cannot even imagine. He is the one who presents our case before God, and we are welcomed in.

God is a gracious Father, but if you don't have a good example of that on earth, you may struggle to relate to him. Jesus is the friend that sticks closer than a brother. Go to him, and bring him all of you.

Pray directly to Jesus today.

PURSUIT OF GODLINESS

You, Timothy, are a man of God; so run from all these evil things. Pursue righteousness and a godly life, along with faith, love, perseverance, and gentleness.

1 TIMOTHY 6:11 NLT

A good Christian holds secret communication with heaven. Private prayer keeps up the trade of godliness. When private holiness is laid aside, a stab is given to the heart of piety.
—Thomas Watson, The Godly Man's Picture

The more we develop our connection with the vine, that is Jesus, the more we pursue godliness in our lives. The virtues of God's kingdom are clear. Pursue righteousness, faith, love, perseverance, and gentleness. Be a pursuer of peace and a harbinger of justice. Do good, be compassionate, and live in integrity.

Sound like too much? Shake off the expectation of perfection. We seek Jesus first and foremost, and he embodies all these things and more. He is our righteousness. He empowers us to choose his grace. When we fail, we repent, and he shakes the dust of shame off and leads us on.

Run toward the things of God's kingdom, not necessarily the easy things, but the right ones.

FULL FELLOWSHIP

That you also may have fellowship with us; and truly our fellowship is with the Father and with His Son Jesus Christ.

1 John 1:3 NKJV

We do not forget to eat: we do not forget to take the shop shutters down: we do not forget to be diligent in business: we do not forget to go to our beds to rest: but we often do forget to wrestle with God in prayer, and to spend, as we ought to spend, long periods in consecrated fellowship with our Father and our God.
—C. H. Spurgeon, The Golden Key of Prayer

Prayer is as urgent to our spiritual health as sleep to our bodies. We eat, we work, we rest, but do we also pray? Prayer is not only about petitioning God for what we need. It isn't even about always doing. There are times to wrestle with the Lord, and there are times to sit peacefully in his presence.

Think of it this way: you have different kinds of interactions with those closest to you. The same will be true of your relationship with God. Some days, you may feel overwhelmed with love, and others you may struggle to understand where he's coming from. The important thing is to stay connected.

Choose to connect to God today.

PERFECT PEACE

You will keep in perfect peace
those whose minds are steadfast,
because they trust in you.
ISAIAH 26:3 NIV

Let it be your business to keep your mind in the presence of the Lord. If it sometimes wander and withdraw itself from Him, do not much disquiet yourself for that: trouble and disquiet serve rather to distract the mind than to re-collect it: the will must bring it back in tranquility. —Brother Lawrence, The Practice of the Presence of God

How often do we berate ourselves for not doing things perfectly? God does not expect perfection. In fact, he doesn't expect excellence one hundred percent of the time, either. Give yourself a break—God does!

He knows who you are, so you can relax. Find your mind wandering during prayer? No big deal! Simply, bring your attention and thoughts back to the Lord. You might even try bringing the very thing that wandered into your thoughts back to him and ask his perspective about it. Keep turning your mind to the Lord, and you will find clarity and rest.

Be gracious with your wandering mind. Notice when it wanders, and bring it back to the Lord.

SIMPLY HOLY

Pray then like this:
"Our Father in heaven,
hallowed be your name."
MATTHEW 6:9 ESV

Though in its beginnings prayer is so simple that the feeble child can pray, yet it is at the same time the highest and holiest work to which man can rise. —Andrew Murray, With Christ in the School of Prayer

Prayer is such a simple exercise, anyone can do it. The smallest child can learn to pray. The beautiful part about growing up in Christ is that we never outgrow the need for prayer. As we develop and grow, so does our understanding. Prayer remains the key to connection with God.

When we pray, we recognize the holiness of God. This is why Jesus taught us to start our prayers with this: "Our Father in heaven, hallowed be your name." *Hallowed* means holy. The more we turn to the holy one, the more we open our hearts and lives to him. As his love transforms us, we become holy as he is holy.

If prayer has become complicated for you, return to a childlike attitude. How can you pray simple prayers to bring you back to connection with God?

GOD'S NATURE

LORD, you are kind and forgiving
and have great love for those who call to you.
PSALM 86:5 NCV

Whatever comes into your heart and mind when you think about God is the most important thing about you.
—A.W. Tozer, The Knowledge of the Holy

Our minds and hearts are not stagnant. They don't remain in the same state. We are influenced by all sorts of things—the people around us, the messages we're hearing, the state of the world—and these are just a few! If we find our thoughts about God change from day to day, we have yet to know him well.

We change, and often, but the Lord never does. He is the same yesterday, today, and forever. It is possible to grow in understanding as we get to know him more. We experience his love, and it transforms us. When he becomes the bedrock of our lives, we can come back to his faithful love when we feel the pressures of life pulling us in different directions.

Ask the Lord to re-center you in his peace as you remember his unchanging love.

CONDUITS OF THE SPIRIT

"You will receive power when the Holy Spirit has come on you, and you will be my witnesses in Jerusalem, in all Judea and Samaria, and to the ends of the earth."

ACTS 1:8 CSB

The Holy Ghost does not flow through methods, but through men. He does not come on machinery, but on men. He does not anoint plans, but men—men of prayer. —E. M. Bounds, Power Through Prayer

God is not looking for good systems. He is not waiting for better technology. He created humankind in his image, and it is that very image he moves on and through. The Holy Spirit anoints the people of God as they seek him.

If you've been waiting to step into what God has put on your heart because you don't feel ready, ask yourself if it is truly the timing or fear that is holding you back. If you are waiting for the Spirit's confirmation that is a good place to be. If you have already received it, but you want more of a sign, consider this it. The Holy Spirit doesn't need you to know the way it's all going to work out. Have faith, take that first step, and trust that God will reveal the subsequent steps as you go.

Is there something you've been hesitating on moving forward in that needs your active obedience?

FEAR AS A MOTIVATOR

The fear of the LORD is the beginning of knowledge;
Fools despise wisdom and instruction.
PROVERBS 1:7 NASB

Fear itself will teach us that no time ought to be without prayer.
—John Calvin, Institutes of the Christian Religion

Fear doesn't have to be something that keeps us stuck in fight, flight, or freeze. It can be the signal for us to turn to the Lord in prayer. Fear is a reminder that we are human, but God's perfect peace is the portion of those that call on him. Go to him with your fear. Showing up when you are afraid is called *courage*.

The Lord teaches those who humble themselves before him. He offers wisdom, instruction, and counsel. He leads them by his Spirit. There is nothing you face that God doesn't know how to handle. There is no problem that stumps him. Bring him all of it—the questions, the wonderings of your heart, the hesitations—and he will speak life into them.

Let fear remind you it's time to press in to prayer.

A BIGGER PERSPECTIVE

Even when you ask, you don't get it because your motives are all wrong—you want only what will give you pleasure.
JAMES 4:3 NLT

Why do we pray in the plural, "Give us"? Why is it not said, "Give me?"... It reproves narrow-spirited men who move within their own sphere only; who look only at themselves, and mind not the case of others; who leave others out of their prayers; if they have daily bread, they care not though others starve; if they are clothed, they care not though others go naked. Christ taught us to pray for others, to say, "Give us." —Thomas Watson, The Lord's Prayer

It is important that we not only pray for our own needs. Life or society may have taught us from an early age that survival was the most necessary pursuit. But this is not how we're meant to live. If you didn't have a safe space to grow with healthy parents to guide you and teach you generosity and the beauty of interconnection, you may need to learn how to do that now.

God is the perfect Father. He will provide for you. Your heart will grow as you learn to reach outside of your self-narrative to the larger story and community you are a part of.

Pray for the greater "us" instead of "me" today.

IMMOVABLE TRUST

Not that I speak in regard to need, for I have learned in whatever state I am, to be content.
PHILIPPIANS 4:11 NKJV

The Christian knows no change with regard to God. He may be rich today and poor tomorrow; he may be sickly today and well tomorrow; he may be in happiness today, tomorrow he may be distressed—but there is no change with regard to his relationship to God. If He loved me yesterday, He loves me today. —C. H. Spurgeon, Morning and Evening

Prayerful practices keep our hearts centered on the unchanging one. God is abundant in love, peace, joy, hope, grace, faith, and provision. There is nothing you need that he cannot provide. Though our circumstances change over time, God's faithfulness does not. He is a sure help, no matter the season.

Do you know what's really wonderful about this? It doesn't matter if the trouble we find ourselves in is due to the world, random chance, or if we somehow did it to ourselves. His grace is sufficient, regardless. As long as we are willing to humble ourselves before God and receive his grace, we can know his uninterrupted loving fellowship.

Trust the Lord with this day and everything you will face.

TOTAL SURRENDER

Then Jesus said to his disciples, "Whoever wants to be my disciple must deny themselves and take up their cross and follow me."
MATTHEW 16:24 NIV

That we ought, once for all, heartily to put our whole trust in God.
—Brother Lawrence, The Practice of the Presence of God

If we want to know the power of fellowship with God, it is not a casual thing we opt into. If we want to truly be disciples of Jesus, then it requires commitment. We don't have to dive in from the first moments, but we also can't hesitate on the edges forever.

If we want to know the power of God in and through our lives, it requires submission and total surrender. No more playing it safe on the sidelines. No more claiming to love God but really looking for ways to serve ourselves. Prayer is the place of interchange. Start there. But don't let it end there. Open your heart and life to Christ, and you will live in the abundance of his life-giving mercy.

Have you totally surrendered your life to Christ?

POWER TO BELIEVE

Jesus said to him, "'If you can'! All things are possible for one who believes."
Mark 9:23 esv

The power to believe a promise depends entirely on our faith in the one who promises. —Andrew Murray, With Christ in the School of Prayer

We don't have to make ourselves believe the promise of God. It begins with knowing the one who promised. This is good news for those of us who sometimes struggle to endure in the waiting between promise and fulfillment. If the one who called us and promised is faithful, the weight of responsibility to follow through is on him. And he will!

Let's be sure the focus of our belief is rooted in Christ. If we believe that he is the Son of God, we can more readily receive our adoption into his family. If we believe that Christ died and rose again to defeat sin, shame, and death, the promise of eternal life rests on him. Let's join our belief to Christ, and everything else will stem from that place.

When you waver in belief over a promise, remember the power of the one who promised.

IT'S A PRACTICE

Everyone has sinned and fallen short of God's glorious standard.
ROMANS 3:23 NCV

We must practice living to the glory of God, actually and determinedly. By meditation upon this truth, by talking it over with God often in our prayers, by recalling it to our minds frequently as we move about among men, a sense of its wondrous meaning will begin to take hold of us. —A. W. Tozer, The Pursuit of God

Living to the glory of God is not about doing it perfectly. We cannot will ourselves to do everything right, and God doesn't expect it! The ideal of perfection is an illusion for us living in frail human bodies in a world filled with sorrow, weakness, and trouble.

God is the God of redemption, restoration, and hope. There is nothing we go through that we cannot grow through. By the grace of God, we can experience miracles of mercy in every season. Remember this life with God is all about practice. So, what will you practice today? We go from glory to glory, not from greatness to perfection.

Thank the Lord for being the glorious standard and offering you grace as you continue to practice and grow.

SURE VICTORY

Thanks be to God, who gives us the victory through our Lord Jesus Christ!

1 Corinthians 15:57 CSB

True prayers are born of present trials and present needs. Bread for today is bread enough. Bread given for today is the strongest sort of pledge that there will be bread tomorrow. Victory today is the assurance of victory tomorrow. Our prayers need to be focused upon the present. We must trust God today, and leave the morrow entirely with Him. The present is ours; the future belongs to God. Prayer is the task and duty of each recurring day—daily prayer for daily needs. —E. M. Bounds, The Necessity of Prayer

Yesterday's provisions serve as a testimony of God's faithfulness. If we had what we needed then, we can be assured that we will receive what is needed today.

"Victory today is the assurance of victory tomorrow." The breakthroughs we experience build up our faith and expand what is possible. Though we cannot erase the struggle of certain unexpected troubles, we can rest in the faithful help of God who gets us through.

Ask God to bring to mind a testimony of his faithfulness.

STOP STRIVING

"Stop striving and know that I am God;
I will be exalted among the nations, I will be exalted on the earth."
Psalm 46:10 nasb

Prayer should be the natural outflow of the soul: you should pray because you must pray, not because the set time for praying has arrived, but because your heart must cry unto your Lord.
—C. H. Spurgeon, Prayer, the Proof of Godliness

Stop striving. It's less of a harsh command and more of a gentle invitation. God sees the way you keep pushing through and trying your best. You don't have to prove yourself to him. He invites you to lean back, take a load off, and know that he is God.

Rest in the presence of the one who knows you best. If you want prayer to be a natural outflow of the soul, rest is necessary. God will refresh you as you lie down in the green pastures of his grace. Prayer can be the decision to stop producing and choose to rest your body, heart, and mind in his presence.

Spend time resting in God's love as your prayer today.

LOVELY AND TRUE

Fix your thoughts on what is true, and honorable, and right, and pure, and lovely, and admirable. Think about things that are excellent and worthy of praise.
PHILIPPIANS 4:8 NLT

We must know before we can love. In order to know God, we must often think of Him; and when we come to love Him, we shall then also think of Him often, for our heart will be with our treasure.
—Brother Lawrence, The Practice of the Presence of God

The beauty of God's nature is irresistible. When we catch a glimpse of his affectionate gaze as we look toward our Creator, we cannot help but be captivated by his love. If we want to know God more, to see him in the world around us, we have only to fix our thoughts on what is true, honorable, right, pure, lovely, admirable, excellent, and worthy of praise. Then we will recognize these traits in the world around us.

The more we recognize God's fingerprints, the more our hearts will overflow with gratitude for the one who never leaves us. There is a world of beauty to behold. The more we fix our thoughts on that, the easier we will find the glimmers of God's light in the darkness.

Pray for eyes to see God's thoughtful care in the world.

SET APART

He was there with the Lord forty days and forty nights; he neither ate bread nor drank water. And He wrote on the tablets the words of the covenant, the Ten Commandments.
Exodus 34:28 NKJV

To be alone in secret with the Father: this be your highest joy. To be assured that the Father will openly reward the secret prayer, so that it cannot remain unblessed.
—Andrew Murray, With Christ in the School of Prayer

When we set ourselves apart in the presence of God, especially when we know there is breakthrough required, that time becomes a sacred space of connection and revelation. Moses went up on the mountains alone to be with the Father, and he returned with the Ten Commandments. Jesus went out into the wilderness for forty days, and came back with the power of God.

Some seasons all we can offer God is our mornings or evenings for prayer. A little bit each day keeps the cup filled. There are times when more is required of us to be alone in God. These are perhaps once-in-a-lifetime opportunities, but they are never wasted.

Set apart devoted time to be alone with God.

AS YOU ARE

Cast your cares on the Lord
and he will sustain you.
Psalm 55:22 NIV

If when we come to prayer our hearts feel dull and unspiritual, we should not try to argue ourselves out of it. Rather, we should admit it frankly and pray our way through. —A.W. Tozer, The Root of Righteousness

We don't have to pretend to be anything but what we are in the moment. If we are tired, let us admit it to the Lord. If we're feeling resistant to spending time with God, let's be honest about it! God isn't afraid of our weakness. He knows us better than we know ourselves, and he welcomes us into his presence with love, grace, and peace.

In order to cast your cares on the Lord, you need to know what they are. If you keep dismissing them, they will not go away. Their weight may grow in the shadows of your heart, mind, and body. Bring them out into the light and offer them to your Savior today. God doesn't just want you on your best days. He wants you as you are now.

Be honest in your prayers today.

CREATIVE FORCE

By faith we understand that the universe was created by the word of God, so that what is seen was not made out of things that are visible.
Hebrews 11:3 ESV

God shapes the world by prayer. —E. M. Bounds, Purpose in Prayer

God is our Creator, the shaper of everything we see, and know, and touch. He is behind the mysteries we cannot grasp, and he is continually creating. The fact that our universe keeps expanding is testimony of this creative force.

What God does, he does exceedingly well. You don't have to simply sit back and watch. You can help shape what is coming by partnering with God's heart in your prayers. Pray for those who need help. Extend your prayers to include those on the other side of the world. Keep praying for the work of the Lord to go forth and reveal his power, majesty, and incomparable love.

Let creativity fill your prayers as you join with God's heart in intercession today.

GIVE THANKS

Let them give thanks to the LORD for his love
and for the miracles he does for people.
He satisfies the thirsty and fills up the hungry.
PSALM 107:8-9 NCV

Here we are, getting blessings from God day after day; yet how little praise and thanksgiving there is in the Church.
—D. L. Moody, Prevailing Prayer

A prayer life without thanks is like a car with the emergency brake on. Trying to move ahead, we feel that resistance. However, when we enter God's presence with thanksgiving and praise, the way opens, and we find ourselves cruising right into the throne room of grace.

We don't have to look far to find reasons to be grateful. If we have food in our bellies, loved ones who support us, a roof over our heads, and work to do, we have an abundance of reasons to praise the Lord. The more we practice gratitude, the more we see the little glimmers of goodness around us. With awe, we pour out our hearts in praise.

Spend time in thanksgiving and praise today.

WELL-ROUNDED

Pray also for me, that the message may be given to me when I open my mouth to make known with boldness the mystery of the gospel... Pray that I might be bold enough to speak about it as I should.

EPHESIANS 6:19-20 CSB

"With all prayer (Ephesians 6:18)." All sorts of prayer—public, private, mental, vocal. Do not be diligent in one kind of prayer and negligent in others... let us use all.
—John Wesley, Explanatory Notes Upon the New Testament

A well-rounded prayer life does not get stuck on one or two types of prayer. Let us evaluate what we spend the most time praying about. Where we have strong tendencies, perhaps it's time to round out our spiritual connection in other ways.

We may readily thank God for his goodness, but perhaps we need to also make room for repentance. We may list off our needs before God and ignore the opportunities to meet those of the people around us out of the abundance we already have. Perhaps our prayers are mostly personal and don't include intercession for others. There is room to grow in our prayer lives always. Take this opportunity to strengthen the weaker areas by God's grace.

Pray for perspective to help you grow in your prayer life.

GOD'S GRACIOUS GIFTS

Not that we are adequate in ourselves so as to consider anything as having come from ourselves, but our adequacy is from God.
2 Corinthians 3:5 nasb

Let nothing disturb thee, nothing affright thee. All things are passing. God never changeth, patient endurance. Attaineth to all things, who God possesseth. In nothing is wanting; alone God sufficeth.
—St. Teresa of Ávila, The Life of Teresa of Jesus

We have all we need in fellowship with the Lord. Even those needs that have yet to be met find their sufficiency in him. He is the source of everything good. Everything we go through in this life is temporary, but God is eternally good. He is forever faithful. He is, and he was, and he always will be.

Give God your time and attention today. Give him your heart, your worries, and your gratitude. Offer him the vulnerable places in your life, and trust him to care tenderly for those things. You are not alone; you have the Source of life as your very near and present help.

Turn St. Teresa's prayer into your own.

HE CAN'T REFUSE

Having chosen them, he called them to come to him. And having called them, he gave them right standing with himself. And having given them right standing, he gave them his glory.
ROMANS 8:30 NLT

Groanings which cannot be uttered are often prayers which cannot be refused. —C. H. Spurgeon, The Treasury of David

You know what God can't refuse? A heart that reaches out to him with genuine interest and need. He is the one who chose us first. He called us before we knew him. He offered right standing through Christ. More than that, he gives us his glory. Everything that we long for—the groans of prayers we don't even know how to put into words—is planted by God. Of course he won't refuse!

When you consider all that God has done for you and the love he has for you, why do you hesitate in trusting his provision? If you have any inkling in your heart toward the Lord today, it is evidence that God is drawing you to him. Follow it. Let your inner longings lead you to him.

Trust that the prayers you don't know how to pray are still being heard.

PRACTICE THE PRESENCE

When You said, "Seek My face,"
My heart said to You, "Your face, Lord, I will seek."
Psalm 27:8 NKJV

I cannot imagine how religious persons can live satisfied without the practice of the presence of God. For my part I keep myself retired with Him in the depth of centre of my soul as much as I can; and while I am so with Him I fear nothing; but the least turning from Him is insupportable. —Brother Lawrence, The Practice of the Presence of God

The practice of the presence of God is the habit of turning our attention to the Lord in prayer, recognizing his nearness through his Spirit. We are seen, known, and heard by the God who draws us to himself in lovingkindness.

Sometimes we need a nudge, and the Lord knows that. "Seek my face," he says. And we get to respond, "Your face, Lord, will I seek." Communion with God is more than talking at God. It is a practice of listening and responding to his voice. The more we respond to his invitations, the more we practice his presence in our lives.

Listen and respond to God's voice today.

CHILDREN OF GOD

See what great love the Father has lavished on us, that we should be called children of God! And that is what we are! The reason the world does not know us is that it did not know him.

1 JOHN 3:1 NIV

The power of prayer depends almost entirely upon our apprehension of who it is with whom we speak.
—Andrew Murray, With Christ in the School of Prayer

When we know our place before the Father as his children, we are given boldness before his throne. A beloved child does not have to hesitate in their parent's presence. They can go to them freely, and they will be received with delight and care.

As God's children we get to know him personally. We get to see his goodness up close. The more we grow in him, the more fully we see his beauty, wisdom, and grace. This is the way the power of prayer is meant to blossom—through fellowship with our Father.

Pray as a beloved child approaching their heavenly Father.

TIME WELL SPENT

Keep yourselves in the love of God, waiting for the mercy of our Lord Jesus Christ that leads to eternal life.

Jude 1:21 ESV

No shortcut exists. God has not bowed to our nervous haste nor embraced the methods of our machine age. It is well that we accept the hard truth now: The man who would know God must give time to Him. He must count no time wasted which is spent in the cultivation of His acquaintance. —A.W. Tozer, The Root of Righteousness

It seems we're all in a hurry these days. This has not always been the case. In fact, we can find much slower paces of living still in certain parts of the world. While we glorify the frenzy of activity and productivity, God is not impressed by these things. He's not in a hurry.

What it would do to our prayer lives if we learned to slow down and savor the present goodness of God. In a world where information is readily at our fingertips, we've forgotten the power of patience. We can learn this in God's presence. Time is not wasted when it's spent in God's fellowship. Not a minute of it! Let's give him our time and trust him with what needs to get done outside of it.

Slow down in prayer today and savor a slower pace.

BE THE BRIDGE

It pleases God our Savior, who wants all people to be saved and to know the truth.
1 Timothy 2:3-4 NCV

Around us is a world lost in sin, above us is a God willing and able to save; it is ours to build the bridge that links heaven and earth, and prayer is the mighty instrument that does the work.
—E. M. Bounds, Power Through Prayer

What a powerful privilege it is to pray for God's kingdom to come to earth in tangible ways. Prayer is the bridge that brings heaven to earth, and it is one we need not take for granted. Every problem faced is an opportunity to invite God's fullness to meet it.

We do not only pray for ourselves. There are people around us in need. There are many people suffering even now. How can we help them? Let's keep our eyes open for ways to be the hands and feet of Jesus through support and generosity. But let's not look helplessly on when we don't know what else to do. We can pray! That's where clarity comes, where deliverance flows, and where answers are given.

Pray for God's fullness to come to situations and people that need it today.

BOUND UP IN LOVE

"I give you a new command: Love one another. Just as I have loved you, you are also to love one another."
John 13:34 CSB

Our prayer must not be self-centered. It must arise not only because we feel our own need as a burden we must lay upon God, but also because we are so bound up in love for our fellow men that we feel their need as acutely as our own. To make intercession for men is the most powerful and practical way in which we can express our love for them.
—John Calvin, Institutes of the Christian Religion

What would it look like to feel the need of the people around us as acutely as we feel our own? It would not be a burden that has no outlet, for we can take every need to the Lord in prayer. Let's not be so micro-focused on our own lives that we fail to consider the needs of those around us.

When was the last time you listened to a personal story that moved you? Take time to ask questions of those in your life. Pay attention to the needs presented, and do what you can to meet them. More than anything, turn them over to the King of kings.

Pray for a specific need someone around you has today.

VESSELS OF PRAYER

"I will give you a new heart and put a new spirit within you; and I will remove the heart of stone from your flesh and give you a heart of flesh. And I will put My Spirit within you and bring it about that you walk in My statutes, and are careful and follow My ordinances."
Ezekiel 36:26-27 NASB

Prayer for the work will soon arouse your own sympathy and effort.
—D. L. Moody, Men of the Bible

When we pray, it is often we who are changed. We don't know how we should pray, but we do it anyway. We see a need, and we start praying. Soon, our hearts are filled with love and passion to see that need met. Sometimes, God moves our hearts to be the very answer we're praying for.

God's Spirit at work in us is what gives us the energy, motivation, and desire to walk in the ways of Christ and to do what he says. The more we pray for God's kingdom to come, the more passionate we become about being that change in the world.

Pray for a need you see today until your heart is transformed.

DEVOTED HEARTS

"Not everyone who calls out to me, 'Lord! Lord!' will enter the Kingdom of Heaven. Only those who actually do the will of my Father in heaven will enter."

MATTHEW 7:21 NLT

How can you expect to dwell with God forever, if you so neglect and forsake him here?
—Jonathan Edwards, Hypocrites Deficient in the Duty of Prayer

Devoted hearts are revealed by devoted lives. A casual relationship with God might make our hearts feel better in small increments, but a life that is enveloped in the love of God cannot be mistaken.

A life lived before the Lord and in line with the values of his kingdom is never wasted. Few on this earth may recognize or know you, but God sees, knows, and honors the legacy you leave. Choose him, not because you have to (you don't), but because God's ways are better than you can imagine. His love is worth it every time—even and especially when it is a sacrifice.

Press into the place of prayer today for no other reason than to know Jesus more.

UNTROUBLED

"Let not your heart be troubled; you believe in God, believe also in Me."
John 14:1 NKJV

If you can trust Him with your soul, you must of necessity trust Him with your prayers! —C. H. Spurgeon, Prayer Certified of Success

Trust does not always come easily. When we feel the pressures of life rising, trust is a vulnerable choice. It takes courage to look in the face of unknowns and say, "I don't know how this will turn out, but I trust the one who does."

You can trust God with your soul. He is eternal, and in him you find eternal life. This is no small matter! He is the Creator of it all, so why would we let our hearts tremble over the empty threats of powerless men? We can trust the faithfulness of our God who never changes. He gives light, life, and hope to all who dwell in him.

Put your full trust in God as you offer him your worries, cares, and specific needs.

BY DAY BY NIGHT

By day the Lord went ahead of them in a pillar of cloud to guide them on their way and by night in a pillar of fire to give them light, so that they could travel by day or night. Neither the pillar of cloud by day nor the pillar of fire by night left its place in front of the people.

Exodus 13:21-22 NIV

Think often on God, by day, by night, in your business and even in your diversions. He is always near you and with you; leave him not alone. —Brother Lawrence, The Practice of the Presence of God

When we think often of God, our attention is drawn to God's nearness. Just as he was with the Israelites in the desert, he goes with us. No matter what we're doing—whether talking with a friend, walking the dog, or doing our work—it all can be done with the company of God.

Even the smallest task becomes more enjoyable as we bring God into it. We do not bother God with reaching out to him. We can't annoy him. He delights in his people drawing near, and he always comes close in return.

Invite God into everyday life with you.

THE FATHER WAITS

"I will strengthen you, I will help you,
I will uphold you with my righteous right hand."
Isaiah 41:10 ESV

O my Lord! Strengthen my faith so in the Father's tender love and kindness, that as often as I feel sinful or troubled, the first instinctive thought may be to go where I know the Father waits me, and where prayer never can go unblessed. Let the thought that He knows my need before I ask, bring me, in great restfulness of faith, to trust that He will give what His child requires. —Andrew Murray, Teach Us to Pray

There is a place for you in God's presence where the Father waits for you. He is always drawing you to himself. Whenever you turn to face him, the light of his love shines upon you. This is the place where you are strengthened in faith.

God knows exactly what you need before you even think to ask him. In great restfulness of faith, trust that he will give what his child requires. You can with confidence and peace approach the throne of grace at any time. Receive his love, and rest in his faithfulness.

Turn toward the Father in prayer, knowing he waits for you.

THE BEST YOU CAN

In all the work you are doing, work the best you can. Work as if you were doing it for the Lord, not for people.
COLOSSIANS 3:23 NCV

As Christians, we can turn some of the most hopeless jobs into wonderful spiritual prayer meetings, if we will simply turn them over to God. —A.W. Tozer, Of God and Men

The best you can do does not equal perfect. If you're energy is low and you do the best you can with what you have in the moment, it is enough. Release your unrealistic expectations and offer what you have to the Lord. He receives it gladly, and he puts his strength behind it.

If God is the one you're looking to honor with your life, you don't have to be afraid of taking the time to rest. In fact, look at your life to see if you are embracing rhythms of rest by taking a Sabbath as God showed us by his example. Join your work—the mundane, the difficult, the boring, the exciting, the unknown—with God, and rest in his honoring of it.

Offer God the work of your hands today, and invite him into all you do.

A BETTER GIFT

If the eagerness is there, the gift is acceptable according to what a person has, not according to what he does not have.
2 CORINTHIANS 8:12 CSB

It is not great talents nor great learning nor great preachers that God needs, but men great in holiness, great in faith, great in love, great in fidelity, great for God -- men always preaching by holy sermons in the pulpit, by holy lives out of it. —E. M. Bounds, Power Through Prayer

The gift of our hearts is what God is after. He wants us to be so yielded to him that we unfold in the light of his love as we were always meant to. In growth, we unfurl our self-protective armor and dare to expand and bloom.

Talent can get easy attention. People love talented individuals! But the gift is not what makes us worthy of love. It's not what makes us children of God. Our identity as children of God is in us already. A good parent doesn't force their child to become a cook, a businessman, or a musician. A good parent helps direct the child to grow, uncover, and steward what is in them. Let's allow ourselves the same leisure in God.

Put God first, and your growth will reveal the power of his love at work in you.

REASON TO REJOICE

"For God so loved the world, that He gave His only Son, so that everyone who believes in Him will not perish, but have eternal life."
John 3:16 nasb

Even if nothing else called for thankfulness, it would always be an ample cause for it that Jesus Christ loved us, and gave Himself for us. —D. L. Moody, Sovereign Grace

The sacrifice Jesus Christ made on the cross so we could know God, be cleansed of unrighteousness, and be welcomed into the eternal kingdom of the Father is beyond a brief note of thanks. Every time we think of it, let us turn in thankfulness and praise.

Even if life is hard at the moment and we cannot readily find reasons to rejoice, let this one still cause our hearts to sing: God so loved the world that he gave his only Son, so that whoever believes in him will not perish, but have eternal life. This is reason to rejoice, indeed!

Worship the Lord in gratitude for his gift of salvation.

SEEK GOD FIRST

"Seek the Kingdom of God above all else, and he will give you everything you need."
Luke 12:31 NLT

In using all means, seek God alone. In and through every outward thing, look only to the power of His Spirit, and the merits of His Son. Beware you do not get stuck in the work itself; if you do, it is all lost labor. Nothing short of God can satisfy your soul. Therefore, fix on Him in all, through all, and above all. —John Wesley, The Means of Grace

When we seek God first, he becomes the foundation of every good thing we receive. He becomes our counselor when we are planning which next step to take. He is the friend when we need a boost of support. He is the truth teller when we are out of line. He is the source of strength when we are weak. In all means, he is able to meet us.

Work is not a bad thing. It is part of what we were made to do. But it is just a part. Rest is also imperative. But that is not all we do, either. Whenever we turn our attention to the Lord and seek him above the work and above the rest, we can more clearly see where he is in everything.

Seek God for perspective in every area of your life.

HIS ANSWER

Then you shall call, and the LORD will answer;
You shall cry, and He will say, "Here I am."
ISAIAH 58:9 NKJV

When God, in answer to their prayers and succeeding their endeavours, delivers, restores, and advances his church, according to his promise, then he is said to answer, and come, and say, Here am I, and to show himself; and they are said to find him, and see him plainly. —Jonathan Edwards, An Humble Attempt

When we cry out to God, he answers. When we cannot sense it, let's keep pursuing him and trusting that his reply will come. Though simple, it is profound to know that he is with us in all we go through.

God is our great deliverer, our mighty restorer, advancer of his salvation truth, and faithful to fulfill his promises. There is nothing he does not do exceedingly well. We can trust him as we pursue him. He will come through for us, just as he has for generations before and those to come. He is with us. We have only to cry out, and he will answer, "Here I am."

Listen for God's reply as you pray.

GO TO THE HILLS

After removing Saul, he made David their king. God testified concerning him: "I have found David son of Jesse, a man after my own heart; he will do everything I want him to do."
Acts 13:22 NIV

Those dark and silent hills provided a suitable prayer chapel for the Son of God. —C. H. Spurgeon, Morning and Evening

David was known as a man after God's own heart. What an incredible thing to be known for! He might have been a mighty king of Israel, but he started out as a God-loving shepherd boy. It was on the hills where he walked with God that he learned to love him. It was out of this intimacy with God that he had the courage to fight off a lion and bear. It was out of this confident relationship that David took on Goliath when the army of Israel would not dare.

Not only was David's faith formed in nature, but the fellowship of Jesus with his heavenly Father also happened when he retreated to the hills to pray. During his ministry, Jesus always made it a priority to go off on his own to cultivate his alone time with the Father.

Bring your prayer time outside and expect God to meet you there.

SO VERY NEAR

The LORD is near to all who call on him,
to all who call on him in truth.
PSALM 145:18 ESV

That we need only to recognize GOD intimately present with us, to address ourselves to Him every moment, that we may beg His assistance for knowing His will in things doubtful, and for rightly performing those which we plainly see He requires of us, offering them to Him before we do them, and giving Him thanks when we have done.
—Brother Lawrence, The Practice of the Presence of God

One of the greatest gifts of knowing God is knowing him in his nearness. The presence of God draws close in tangible peace through the Holy Spirit. We have only to draw our attention to God, to recognize him intimately present with us.

Every moment is an opportunity to turn our attention to the Lord, and as we do, give him our hearts, our minds, and our ears. Prayer becomes as intimate as a conversation with a close friend. God is always ready to meet us as we are and with all that we need. Let's invite him into the details of our day as we practice continually reaching out to him.

Turn to God casually throughout your day to connect through prayer.

WORSHIP HIM

"The time is coming when the true worshipers will worship the Father in spirit and truth, and that time is here already. You see, the Father too is actively seeking such people to worship him."
JOHN 4:23 NCV

Many confess to a lack of a deep spiritual life, and many prayers for its deepening are made. Yet there is often ignorance as to what is needed to bring a foundering Christian to a strong and joyous life in Christ. Nothing can meet our need better than the adoring worship of the Holy Trinity. —Andrew Murray, Power in Prayer

If we want to deepen our relationship with God, there are ways to do that. It is through adoration of the Father, Son, and Spirit that we experience strength and joy in our inner world. If we want more joy, let's worship him! If we want more strength, let's adore who God is for all that he was, is, and will be!

God is worthy of praise, not because he says so, but because of what he consistently proves through his character. Let's not become so caught up in the needs we have, the work that is yet to be done, or the demands of others that we miss out on the beauty of our God.

Spend time in worship and let your heart connect to the giver of life today!

WITH ALL YOU ARE

Love the LORD your God with all your heart, with all your soul, and with all your strength.
DEUTERONOMY 6:5 CSB

To love God with all our heart we must first of all will to do so. We should repent our lack of love and determine from this moment on to make God the object of our devotion. We should set our affections on things above and aim our hearts toward Christ and heavenly things. We should read the Scriptures devotionally every day and prayerfully obey them, always firmly willing to love God with all our heart and our neighbor as ourself. —A. W. Tozer, The Root of Righteousness

Lack of love is at the core of most sin. Praying for more of God's love to flood our minds, hearts, bodies, and lives is a powerful request. Love is not weak—it is the strongest force in the universe. It is the very essence of all that God is.

If we want to love more, we have to choose it. Invite God to transform you as you surrender to his love. As it floods you, you will be able to love him, love others, and love the world more fully.

How can you choose to open your heart to more love today?

ENDURANCE NEEDED

Blessed is a man who perseveres under trial; for once he has been approved, he will receive the crown of life which the Lord has promised to those who love Him.

James 1:12 NASB

No man can do a great and enduring work for God who is not a man of prayer. —E. M. Bounds, Power Through Prayer

Prayer is vital for us to continue in the faith. It keeps our hearts connected and open to God. It is the channel of strength for us to trade our sorrows for God's joy. We trade our anxiety for his peace. We trade our weakness for his strength. We trade our indifference for his love. What glorious and divine exchanges happen in prayer!

Endurance is needed in deep, spiritual work. If we give up when the going gets a little tough, we also give up on the fruit that lies beyond the trial. Perseverance is necessary. In all the things required, we can find strength to continue through prayer.

Trade your limits for God's abundance in prayer today.

COMMUNION OF LOVE

"I have loved you even as the Father has loved me. Remain in my love."

John 15:9 NLT

If our spiritually dead ones are to be raised, we must first get power with God. The reason we so often fail in moving our fellowmen is that we try to win them without first getting power with God. Jesus was in communion with His Father, and so He could be assured that His prayers were heard. —D. L. Moody, Prevailing Prayer

God's power is not the end we seek. The power of God reveals a greater thing: his love. Jesus learned to remain in the Father's love, and we must do the same. To know God closely is to dwell in the power of his love.

Every miracle Jesus performed was a miracle of mercy. God's goodness, his kindness, and his power was revealed through each one. If we want to see the lives of those around us transformed by the mercy of Christ, we must also yield our lives to his incredible fellowship and leadership. Let's not seek to change others before we, ourselves, are changed in his presence.

Spend time remaining in God's love today.

GIVING THANKS

In everything give thanks; for this is the will of God in Christ Jesus for you.
1 Thessalonians 5:18 NKJV

Thanksgiving is inseparable from true prayer; it is almost essentially connected with it. One who always prays is ever giving praise, whether in ease or pain, both for prosperity and for the greatest adversity. He blesses God for all things, looks on them as coming from Him, and receives them for His sake.
—John Wesley, Explanatory Notes Upon the New Testament

Thanksgiving is a powerful practice to align our hearts with the reality of God's goodness. The more we thank him, the more receptive our hearts become. This is a season of thanksgiving, and it is a perfect opportunity to focus our hearts on what is already good, gracious, and worthy of praise.

In everything, give thanks. A sacrifice of praise realigns our perspectives with the faithfulness of God as we choose to give thanks in the face of hardship. When we learn to set aside our preferences and choose gratitude, a shift happens in our hearts. We expand in love.

Give God thanks for the hard things, as well as the good.

FIND REST

"Bring my sons from afar
and my daughters from the ends of the earth…
whom I formed and made."
Isaiah 43:6-7 niv

Thou hast made us for thyself, O Lord, and our heart is restless until it finds its rest in thee. —St. Augustine, Confessions

Though some seasons of life feel as though we're wandering, we don't ever have to feel that way when it comes to God. Through Christ, every distance and barrier has been demolished, and we have access to our heavenly Father through him. He is our home, and our hearts find rest in him.

Access to your true spiritual home is as accessible as the breath you are taking right now. Pray, and ask for the peace of God to flood your being. Pray, and ask your Father to reveal the love he has for you. Go ahead, enter in and make yourself at home in his presence, for he has made his home in you.

Pray for the true rest that comes from knowing God to fill your heart, mind, and body.

THERE'S ROOM

"In my Father's house are many rooms. If it were not so, would I have told you that I go to prepare a place for you?"
JOHN 14:2 ESV

Did you ever stop to think that God is going to be as pleased to have you with Him in Heaven as you are to be there?
—A.W. Tozer, The Knowledge of the Holy

God planned his kingdom to include all who would ever come to him. His love is expansive, and so is heaven. We won't be stuck like sardines in a can. There is plenty of room to spare! Jesus' words are like comfort to our hearts. He was speaking to everyone who would come to him in faith and accept him as their Savior.

God delights in you more than you know. His love for you goes beyond a nominal admiration. He knows you deeply, and he loves you like a proud parent loves their beloved child.

Pray and ask God for a deeper revelation of his delight today.

PRICELESS TREASURE

"The kingdom of heaven is like a treasure hidden in a field. One day a man found the treasure, and then he hid it in the field again. He was so happy that he went and sold everything he owned to buy that field."
Matthew 13:44 NCV

How happy we would be if we could find the treasure of which the Gospel speaks; all else would be as nothing. As it is boundless, the more you search for it the greater the riches you will find; let us search unceasingly and let us not stop until we have found it.
—Brother Lawrence, The Practice of the Presence of God

The treasure of God's kingdom is not fool's gold. It doesn't appear to be costly on the surface but cheap metal inside. It is priceless. We cannot know the full extent of God's abundant kingdom, but it is worth giving all we have to get it.

The kingdom of God is continually expanding. The more you search for it, the greater the riches you will find. There is no limit to the beauty you can uncover as you look for it.

Search for God in prayer and as you move about your day.

SPIRITUAL WORK

There are different gifts, but the same Spirit. There are different ministries, but the same Lord.
1 Corinthians 12:4-5 CSB

The measure of believing and continued prayer will be the measure of the Spirit's working in the church. Direct, definite, and determined prayer is what we need.
—Andrew Murray, The Ministry of Intercession

What comes to mind when you hear the term "spiritual work"? Is it ministry? Perhaps it's serving the poor. Spiritual work is not reserved for those who serve in churches. It's not only for those who pursue God in formal settings. Spiritual work is the work we do empowered by the Spirit.

We each have a different role to play, and we also have unique work that we can invite God into. Continue to pray and yield your time, your talents, and your service to the Lord through a surrendered heart. He will show you what to do and when. Stay connected to him and offer him your work and partnership. He will do the rest.

Ask the Spirit to empower the work you are doing.

SHOWERS OF BLESSING

"I will make them and the places around My hill a blessing. And I will make showers fall in their season; they will be showers of blessing."

EZEKIEL 34:26 NASB

Prayer is always the preface to blessing.
—C. H. Spurgeon, Prayer: The Forerunner of Mercy

If we want to see showers of blessing in our lives, our communities, and in the world, we cannot neglect the power of prayer. Prayer keeps us connected to God and open to receive his grace, goodness, power, and mercy. There is greater awareness of God's bountiful provision when we knock on the door of heaven each day.

A blessing to one might be completely overlooked by another. What is important to you is important to God. He will shower his blessing over you as you pray. You pray and ask, and he sends the rains. Let the soil of your heart soak up the goodness of his love even today!

Where do you need a refreshing rain to meet a dry area in your life?

KNOCK AND ASK

We will receive from him whatever we ask because we obey him and do the things that please him.

1 JOHN 3:22 NLT

The strongest one in Christ's kingdom is he who is the best knocker. The secret of success in Christ's Kingdom is the ability to pray. The one who can wield the power of prayer is the strong one, the holy one in Christ's Kingdom. The most important lesson we can learn is how to pray.
—E. M. Bounds, The Weapon of Prayer

The most important lesson we can learn is how to pray. Jesus did not make it complicated for us. He taught his followers how they should approach God in prayer. If you need a back-to-basics lesson, go there. If you need a refresher or a reset to a simpler prayer life, return there.

If you want to use that as a springboard for a deeper prayer life, knock on the door of heaven with your heartfelt prayer and bring God all that you are. Don't hold back a thing. The more you pray, the more you draw near to the one who knows you best.

Make prayer a practice you come back to throughout your day.

LIFT UP HOLY HANDS

I desire therefore that the men pray everywhere, lifting up holy hands, without wrath and doubting.

1 TIMOTHY 2:8 NKJV

To make intercession for men is the most powerful and practical way in which we can express our love for them.
—John Calvin, Institutes of the Christian Religion

The ministry of intercession is a powerful one. The more we practice praying for others, the more natural it becomes. We should not keep our prayer lives only about us. The kingdom of God is built upon love—for God and others. Inviting our hearts to join to God's in passionate prayer for others will only grow our love for the people around us.

Let's put down our excuses for why we shouldn't pray and see those instead as the very reason we should. If we have hesitation in our hearts, we probably need the love of God to transform our hearts. What better place to do that than in prayer?

Pray for the people who you'd rather keep your distance from.

GREATEST ROMANCE

I am my beloved's and my beloved is mine.
SONG OF SONGS 6:3 NIV

To fall in love with God is the greatest romance; to seek him the greatest adventure; to find him, the greatest human achievement. —St. Augustine, Confessions

The greatest romance in this life is falling in love with God. His love is perfect, and it perfectly meets our needs. We don't just have physical needs that he meets with his provision. We have emotional and spiritual needs that he fills with the power of his love.

There are other kinds of love in this life, but each one is only a glimpse of the goodness of his perfect love. He is the perfect parent, the perfect friend, and the perfect partner. He does not disappoint, and he doesn't misunderstand us; he knows us best and has no need to withhold himself from us.

Ask the Lord to reveal the kindness, specificity, and excitement of his love.

ABSOLUTE SURRENDER

Do not be conformed to this world, but be transformed by the renewal of your mind, that by testing you may discern what is the will of God, what is good and acceptable and perfect.
ROMANS 12:2 ESV

A good conscience is complete obedience to God day by day, and fellowship with God every day in His Word, and prayer—that is a life of absolute surrender. —Andrew Murray, Absolute Surrender

Absolute surrender is remaining yielded to God's lordship in our lives. It is a daily practice to submit our hearts to him in prayer and feast on his Word as our daily bread. Fellowship with the Lord is our source of strength, and he guides us as we learn to walk in his ways.

Don't let a misstep keep you from surrendering to him. This is not a practice of perfection, but of permission. You get to come back to him as many times as necessary to reset. He welcomes you always, and he is ready to receive you, no matter how many times you mess up.

Ask for God's love to meet you as you return to him whenever you need to reset in his mercy.

ABUNDANT GRACE

God's grace has made me what I am, and his grace to me was not wasted. I worked harder than all the other apostles. (But it was not I really; it was God's grace that was with me.)
1 Corinthians 15:10 NCV

O my God, since thou art with me, and I must now, in obedience to thy commands, apply my mind to these outward things, I beseech thee to grant me the grace to continue in thy presence; and to this end do thou prosper me with thy assistance, receive all my works, and possess all my affections. —Brother Lawrence, The Practice of the Presence of God

We cannot avoid the responsibilities of life, but we can invite God into them. As we put minds to work, God can be moving in the depths of our heart at the same time. As we invite the Spirit to be with us, he offers us his clarity, strength, and joy. There is no task we are without his grace, especially those we least look forward to doing.

Oh, that we would know the power of God in the mundane aspects of our lives! Then we would see for certain how loved we are, how present God is, and how nothing is wasted in offering our hearts to him.

Invite God into the mundane, and love him through it all.

TRIED AND TESTED

Lord of Armies, testing the righteous
and seeing the heart and mind.
Jeremiah 20:12 CSB

God never uses anyone greatly until He tests them deeply.
—A.W. Tozer, The Root of Righteousness

God sees our hearts and minds. He knows us well. When we have a great desire to be used by him, he does not throw us into situations where we are in over our head. The more we rely on God's guidance and trust his faithfulness, the more we can walk in obedience.

We have a choice to make in each test. It's not that God's people never choose wrongly. It is well-documented that they do. Even Scripture shows us how faulty we are in our response to the Lord. It is a humble heart that brings us close to the Lord, and a repentant person that experiences great growth.

Do you trust God's wisdom and timing in your life?

LEARNING CURVE

Like newborn babies, long for the pure milk of the word, so that by it you may grow in respect to salvation.

1 PETER 2:2 NASB

Prayer is not the fruit of natural talents; it is the product of faith, of holiness, of deeply spiritual character. Men learn to pray as they learn to love. —E. M. Bounds, The Reality of Prayer

No one comes out of the womb knowing how to live as an adult. Jesus had to grow in stature and in wisdom, and he was the Son of God. He submitted himself to the limitations of humanity, and that included the developmental stages of growing up as a boy. If Jesus needed time to grow and learn the things of God, how much more do we?

If we are not very natural at praying, we shouldn't see that as a reason to give up doing it. The most profound practices are built and learned. Even the simpler things of life are strengthened as we do them more.

Start where you are today in prayer and keep practicing it.

APPROVED

May the Lord our God show us his approval
and make our efforts successful.
Psalm 90:17 NLT

Let us practice the fine art of making every work a priestly ministration. Let us believe that God is in all our simple deeds and learn to find Him there. —A.W. Tozer, The Pursuit of God

It is no small thing to invite God to show us his approval in the small things of life. The simplest deeds can be places of encounter, as our expectant hearts remain open to the Lord. Doing the dishes can be a prayer service if we use it that way. Walking the dog can be a ministry of worship as we lift our hearts in praise.

A talk with a friend can open the portals to heaven as we listen with love, weeping with those who weep and rejoicing with those who rejoice. There is nothing God need stay out of, so why not reach out to him in it all?

In all you do today, look with eyes of expectation to see God in it.

FAITH SUPPORT

Moses' hands became heavy; so they took a stone and put it under him, and he sat on it. And Aaron and Hur supported his hands, one on one side, and the other on the other side; and his hands were steady until the going down of the sun.

EXODUS 17:12 NKJV

Moses grew weary, and then his friends assisted him. When at any time your prayer flags, let faith support one hand, and let holy hope uplift the other, and prayer seating itself upon the stone of Israel, the rock of our salvation, will persevere and prevail.
—C. H. Spurgeon, Morning and Evening

When we grow weary in prayer, let's lean on the support of fellow believers. We might lose strength, but that doesn't mean we have to lose the battle. Hope can be the stone under one arm, as we rely on the support of faithful friends to hold up the other.

We do not have to struggle alone. We need each other. This is the way God made things! He set us in communities and in families, and we are there to help one another. Readily help others when their strength is flagging, and let others know when you need their support.

Send a prayer request to someone to hold with you today.

LOOK TO JESUS

I can testify about them that they are zealous for God, but their zeal is not based on knowledge. Since they did not know the righteousness of God and sought to establish their own, they did not submit to God's righteousness.

ROMANS 10:2-3 NIV

Sin is looking for the right thing in the wrong place.
—St. Augustine, Confessions

There are many religious righteous that think they are on the right track, yet they are missing the Savior. They may be zealous about their faith, but that does not mean that their passion is based on truth.

Jesus is the way, the truth, and the life, and he is the one who sets the standard. Spend time reacquainting yourself with the Jesus. Let your passion lead you to him. The righteousness of God is not about establishing our ways on the earth, but on the love of Christ.

Pray for a deeper revelation of God's truth in the person of Christ.

SET YOUR MIND

We all, with unveiled face, beholding the glory of the Lord, are being transformed into the same image from one degree of glory to another. For this comes from the Lord who is the Spirit.
2 Corinthians 3:18 esv

You can see God from anywhere if your mind is set to love and obey Him. —A.W. Tozer, The Pursuit of God

When our hearts are surrendered to Christ, our lives are fully reconciled to God. There is nothing we have to do but yield to his love. It's the most beautiful exchange: we offer God all our weakness, sin, and disappointment, and he offers us the peace of his presence. When we receive his love, we are filled to the brim so that we can not only love him in return, but also obey him.

What our minds are set upon is what we will readily see in the world around us. If we fix our thoughts on the kindnesses of God, we will recognize his mercies as they spring up.

There are blessings upon blessings in the fellowship of God. Love him, obey him, and give thanks continually.

SAFETY IN PRAYER

The LORD gave the people all the land he had promised their ancestors. The people took the land and lived there.
JOSHUA 21:43 NCV

God's people were always safe when their princes were princes in prayer.
—E. M. Bounds, The Weapon of Prayer

There were many kings of Israel, and not all of them were good. Some rebelled against God or simply went their own way, thinking they knew better than the prophets and judges. The best rulers were those who pursued God personally, and it poured over into the way they ruled.

A yielded heart is good soil for safety. We can trust safe people because their character is rooted in integrity and love. Prayer is good for everyone. It promotes humility of the heart and openness to learn. When we seek the Lord in prayer for ourselves, for our communities, the people we work with, and our families, anything is possible. God's promises are what we build our prayers upon.

How does your prayer life affect the way you relate to others or do your job?

ORDINARY GOODNESS

He has told each of you what is good
and what it is the Lord requires of you:
to act justly, to love faithfulness,
and to walk humbly with your God.
Micah 6:8 CSB

The only humility that is really ours is not the humility we try to show before God in prayer, but that which we carry with us and actively live in our ordinary conduct.
—Andrew Murray, Humility: The Beauty of Holiness

We too often overlook the beauty of the ordinary. That is where the nuts and bolts of our habits build and support the greater arc of our lives. It is in the details of our day, the conversations we have, the work we do, and the little acts of service we make time for that our character is revealed.

If we want to do what is required by the Lord, we can't ignore the call of Micah 6:8. Our humility isn't an act or place of begging before God. It is revealed in the way we live and treat each other. Our actions reveal who we deem most important. Let us be known as lovers of God, even by those who we'll never speak to.

Pray for awareness to act in justice, faithfulness, and with a humble heart today.

SPEAK PLAINLY

Do not be quick with your mouth or impulsive in thought to bring up a matter in the presence of God. For God is in heaven and you are on the earth; therefore let your words be few.

ECCLESIASTES 5:2-3 NASB

Ask for it plainly, as before God, who does not regard your fine expressions, and to whom your eloquence and oratory will be less than nothing and vanity. Thou art before the Lord; let thy words be few, but let thy heart be fervent.
—C. H. Spurgeon, Order and Argument in Prayer

The longer we walk with God, the more familiar we become with his nature. The more familiar we are, the less we have to prove. We don't have to talk around an issue. We can do it directly, without flowery words or the impulse to convince him by giving more context.

You don't have to be afraid of God when you pray, just be mindful. Speak to him like you would a trusted teacher and friend. He is a wise counselor, and he will offer you his leadership whenever you ask for it. Instead of working yourself up before him, relax and tell him directly what it is you need.

Let your words be simple, clear, and few in prayer today.

CHOOSING TRUST

Those who know your name trust in you,
for you, O LORD, do not abandon those who search for you.
PSALM 9:10 NLT

I do not mean that every prayer we offer is answered exactly as we desire it to be. Were this the case, it would mean that we would be dictating to God, and prayer would degenerate into a mere system of begging. —E. M. Bounds, The Possibilities of Prayer

We cannot dictate to God the details of how he should answer our prayer. That is merely a guise at control. The uncomfortable truth is that we cannot control how tomorrow will go. We cannot control how God will answer us. We can trust that we will have what we require for every need at the right time.

Prayer is not meant to be like a wish-list. It is not a series of "now, can I have this?" If you've been around children, you know the impulse to ask for more is always there. In the checkout line, on the computer, walking outside, there's always something not yet attained. Yet, it's when we learn to accept what we have with thanks that we can truly enjoy the moment.

Relax into your prayer, offering God thanks, and enjoying his presence.

ENDURING HOPE

Now abide faith, hope, love, these three; but the greatest of these is love.

1 CORINTHIANS 13:13 NKJV

That all things are possible to him who believes, that they are less difficult to him who hopes, they are more easy to him who loves, and still more easy to him who perseveres in the practice of these three virtues. —Brother Lawrence, The Practice of the Presence of God

The virtues of faith, hope, and love will not end when this world passes away. It is to our spiritual strength to abide in them as long as we live. Efforts spent on pursuing faith, holding on to hope, and growing in loving action are never wasted.

Perseverance is needed, not because we have to trudge through life, but because the seasons of life change, and so do we. There are dark nights and harsh economic times. We go through trials and troubles, and we can't avoid them. But we can continue to grow spiritually strong. We do this through staying connected to God and relying on his presence.

What do you need more of today: faith, hope, or love? Ask God to strengthen you.

PAIRED WITH THE SPIRIT

What shall I do? I will pray with my spirit, but I will also pray with my understanding; I will sing with my spirit, but I will also sing with my understanding.

1 CORINTHIANS 14:15 NIV

A shaking hand may as well write a line steadily, as we can keep our hearts fixed in prayer without the Spirit of God.
—Thomas Watson, The Ten Commandments

Any activity can become spiritual if we pair it with the Spirit of God. As we invite his power into our ordinary lives, he transforms us by sowing seeds of the fruit of his kingdom into the details. As we continue to walk with him and partner with his work, we sow those same seeds in the world around us.

Our hearts may not stay focused in prayer alone; they don't need to. We pray with our understanding, but we also pray with the Spirit. We sing with understanding, but we can also sing with our spirit, and the Holy Spirit meets us in that place. There is beauty in the mystery of fellowship with God, and there is power in the peace of it.

Invite the Spirit to join you in the most ordinary tasks.

CREATION DECLARES

The heavens declare the glory of God,
and the sky above proclaims his handiwork.
Psalm 19:1 ESV

Some people, in order to discover God, read books. But there is a great book: the very appearance of created things. Look above you! Look below you! Read it. God, whom you want to discover, never wrote that book with ink. Instead, He set before your eyes the things that He had made. Can you ask for a louder voice than that?
—St. Augustine, The City of God

We can get so caught up in what we have created that we forget to step back and look at the beauty of creation apart from mankind's influence. Nature is wildly beautiful. There are intricacies of systems that no person could dictate. There is more uncovered in the deep seas than we have already discovered. We are relatively new in the exploration of space and all that lies there.

Nature is a powerful place to encounter God. It is he who hung the stars in the sky and set the planets into motion. It was he who made the mountains and the valleys, the seas and land, and everything in them. The created world declares the glory of God!

Join with nature in glorifying God in the beauty of who he is.

READY TO RECEIVE

Remember that you were slaves in Egypt and that the Lord your God brought you out of there by his great power and strength. So the Lord your God has commanded you to rest on the Sabbath day.

Deuteronomy 5:15 NCV

When trust is perfect and without doubt, prayer is simply the outstretched hand, ready to receive.
—E. M. Bounds, The Necessity of Prayer

Perfect trust isn't about knowing the details of what's to come. It's the confidence we have in knowing the one who does. He shapes the future, and he answers the prayers of his people. He fulfills every promise he has made, and he won't stop now.

What does your trust rely on? Do you wait for a sign to truly trust that God is with you? Do you want assurances from him that things will not be too hard? He promises to go with you. Your trust in him gives you courage to keep following after him. The same God who delivered the Israelites from their captives will bring you into your own breakthroughs. Stretch your hand out in prayer to receive what he offers.

Do you trust God more than you need to know specific answers?

CHRIST'S EXAMPLE

"Truly I tell you, the Son is not able to do anything on his own, but only what he sees the Father doing. For whatever the Father does, the Son likewise does these things."
JOHN 5:19 CSB

The heart of the world is breaking under this load of pride and pretense. There is no release from our burden apart from the meekness of Christ. —A.W. Tozer, The Pursuit of God

Far be it from any of us who follow Christ to put ourselves above him or his ways. He did not demand respect or blind obedience from those who followed him. He invited them to come, and they got to choose their response. He led with humility, mercy, and wisdom always.

It is good to realign ourselves in the love of Christ, including in his humble example. He did nothing on his own, but only what he saw the Father doing. What he did, let us do, and so follow in the way of his kingdom.

Whose example are you following? Pray for a humble heart that follows after your Savior.

HOLY TEACHER

"Repent, and each of you be baptized in the name of Jesus Christ for the forgiveness of your sins; and you will receive the gift of the Holy Spirit."
Acts 2:38 NASB

By His Holy Spirit, He has access to our heart, and teaches us to pray by showing us the sin that hinders the prayer, or giving us the assurance that we please God. He teaches, by giving not only thoughts of what to ask or how to ask, but by breathing within us the very spirit of prayer, by living within us as the Great Intercessor.
—Andrew Murray, With Christ in the School of Prayer

For all who repent and are fully submitted to Jesus Christ, they have the gift of the Holy Spirit. The Spirit is not a servant of God; he is God. He has access to our heart, and he teaches us to pray by revealing what's within us. There may be sin that hinders us or an area of worry that needs to be handed over to him.

The Holy Spirit is our teacher. He brings to mind what God promised. The more we learn about God through fellowship, prayer, and reading the Word, the more is stored in us.

Ask the Holy Spirit what today's prayer focus is.

HEARD

Hear me, LORD, and have mercy on me.
Help me, O LORD.
PSALM 30:10 NLT

Because God has already been our help, we can have confidence in Him for the present and the future. Our prayer is, O Lord, be my helper.
—C. H. Spurgeon, Faith's Checkbook

When we have already experienced God's help, our past becomes confidence for the present and future. Every display of God's faithfulness in our lives raises the floor of our faith. Think back on your history with God. How has he come through for you? What promises has he already fulfilled?

God's help is sure. He is the God of unfailing mercy. Whatever you face today, or to come, you can rest assured that God's presence is with you in that very moment. He is sufficient in grace, and his generosity cannot be measured. Lean into his love as you remember just how powerful he is and how incredibly loved you are by him.

Thank God for the specific ways he has helped you in your life.

REJOICE IN THE LIGHT

"These things I have spoken to you, that My joy may remain in you, and that your joy may be full."

JOHN 15:11 NKJV

This joy in God is not like any pleasure found in physical or intellectual satisfaction. Nor is it such as a friend experiences in the presence of a friend. But, if we are to use any such analogy, it is more like the eye rejoicing in light. —St. Augustine, City of God

What exactly does the eye do to rejoice in the light? It simply sees. It does its job—what it was created to do—and looks. The eyes have a system of detecting color, and our brains decipher the rest. If joy in the Lord is like an eye rejoicing in light, then it simply is in the act of being.

What if your joy was fully realized by embracing who God made you to be and living that? What if enjoying what you are already drawn to is enough to fill your soul to worship the Lord? What if that is your great act of praise today?

Delight in the things you love to delight in, and let your joy be full before the Lord.

FASTING FOR BREAKTHROUGH

"When you fast, put oil on your head and wash your face, so that it will not be obvious to others that you are fasting, but only to your Father, who is unseen; and your Father, who sees what is done in secret, will reward you."

MATTHEW 6:17-18 NIV

Bear up the hands that hang down, by faith and prayer; support the tottering knees. Have you any days of fasting and prayer? Storm the throne of grace and persevere therein, and mercy will come down.
—John Wesley, A Plain Account of Christian Perfection

Fasting is a powerful practice to get us relying on God and persevering in prayer for breakthrough. Fasting without prayer is a dietary decision. Fasting with prayer is a spiritual discipline.

Jesus warned that we shouldn't use fasting as a sign of how spiritual we are. It's not for anyone else to be impressed by. It's for God: what we're praying for and the breakthrough we're seeking. Storm the throne of grace, and mercy will meet you. If you have felt stuck, pairing your prayer with fasting may be the push you need to receive what you've been asking for.

Consider fasting a meal and using that time to pray.

NOTHING TOO HARD

Ah, Lord God! It is you who have made the heavens and the earth by your great power and by your outstretched arm! Nothing is too hard for you.

Jeremiah 32:17 esv

Nothing is too hard for prayer because nothing is too hard for God.
—E. M. Bounds

God has no limits. He has no bounds. Nothing is too hard for him. How often do we really pray like this is true? He is the God who created all that we see. His handiwork is in the cells of our bodies and in the atoms that make up the matter around us. His wisdom, power, and glory are on display.

Why would we limit ourselves with God? Prayer is meant to be a practice where we pour our hearts out to him and receive all that he has to offer. It is a divine interchange, and it is powerful enough to change our lives in a moment. One word from God can shift everything.

Pray for the greater things today.

LOVE IS EVERYTHING

If I do not have love, then I am nothing. I may give away everything I have, and I may even give my body as an offering to be burned. But I gain nothing if I do not have love.
1 Corinthians 13:2-3 NCV

We often do not yield ourselves to God in obedience to His commandment to love our fellow men with Christ's love. What if that love should flow out to all around, even to those who hate us? This would require much grace and cost us time and trouble and serious prayer. —Andrew Murray, The Ministry of Intercession

Love is the goal in everything we do in Christ because he is love. If we learn to sip coffee with love, chat with the neighbor with love, and pursue peace with love, we do well. Love is the foundation of all that we seek. It truly doesn't matter what we do if we lack love. It is an empty gesture.

Love is not a theory. It is something we come back to in practice, in intention, and in action. We never grow out of needing to live from love. We are ever-expanding, even as love keeps on growing. Let us look for ways to love in word, in deed, in spirit, and in truth today.

Pray for greater love to fill you, motivate you, and move you.

WONDROUSLY MADE

I will praise you because I have been
remarkably and wondrously made.
Your works are wondrous, and I know this very well.
PSALM 139:14 CSB

Does God proclaim Himself in the wonders of creation? No. All things proclaim Him, all things speak. Their beauty is the voice by which they announce God, by which they sing, "It is you who made me beautiful, not me myself but you. —St. Augustine, Confessions

God has no need to glorify himself in creation. The work of his hands is evidence enough of his glorious wisdom, creativity, and love. We, as his handiwork, are able to offer him praise by joining with creation and singing the song of his glory. Let's give thanks!

It is not pride to recognize how thoughtfully God created you. To recognize his power and thoughtfulness alive in you is to catch a glimpse of his affection for you. You are one of his works, and all of his works are wondrous!

Praise God for how he made you—wondrous and remarkably you!

FAITH WALK

Teach me the way in which I should walk;
For to You I lift up my soul.
PSALM 143:8 NASB

Teach us to know that we cannot know, for the things of God knoweth no man, but the Spirit of God. Let faith support us where reason fails, and we shall think because we believe, not in order that we may believe. —A.W. Tozer, The Knowledge of the Holy

We rely on the Spirit of God to direct us in what we cannot know. There is so much we try to control, but there is very little we actually can. We can choose for ourselves how we will live and act, but beyond that, we have to trust the one who knows better than we ever could.

Trust is necessary in life. Even those without faith trust something. It may be their own ability, their government, or the people around them. As followers of Christ, we get to put our trust in the faithful God who never changes. He is always abundant in love, focused in wisdom, and powerful in redemption.

Pray today's verse, and trust God to meet you.

A DIFFERENT MEASURE

Teach those who are rich in this world not to be proud and not to trust in their money, which is so unreliable. Their trust should be in God, who richly gives us all we need for our enjoyment.

1 TIMOTHY 6:17 NLT

Leaders in the realm of religious activity are to be judged by their praying habits, and not by their money or social position.
—E. M. Bounds, The Weapon of Prayer

We don't have to try hard to judge each other. The inclination is right there. We judge businesses for how they treat their employees. We judge leaders for the decisions they make. We judge each other based on what we think is right. But all of this is pointless. We are called to love each other as Christ loved us and gave himself for us.

The measure of a godly person has nothing to do with what they wear, how much money they have, or their social position. God's kingdom is not made up of classes. We would do well to humble ourselves and readjust our expectations of what it is to be a follower of Christ. Humble, loving, kind, honest, and reliable people are the people we should strive to be.

Pray for a humble heart that gives grace and walks in love.

STILL WORKING

Being confident of this very thing, that He who has begun a good work in you will complete it until the day of Jesus Christ.
PHILIPPIANS 1:6 NKJV

It is a comforting thing to know that the Lord will not begin the good work without also finishing it.
—D. L. Moody, The Way to God and How to Find It

The God who began his good work in you has not stopped. He will continue it until the day of Christ's return. What he has started, he will finish. This is good news! Let out a shout of joy or a deep sigh of relief. You are not done, and God is not done with you.

You can trust God's heart and his Word. He will not go back on it. Lean into his fellowship and ask him to show you what he wants to do in you today. You are in process, and that will always be true. God's love is working in your heart as you yield to him. Let it have its full effect, and keep taking each step as he shows you. You are on your way.

Praise God that he is still at work in you, and ask him to show you how you can partner with his work.

BETTER THAN LIFE

Because your love is better than life,
my lips will glorify you.
PSALM 63:3 NIV

Oh, God, to know you is life. To serve You is freedom. To praise you is the soul's joy and delight. Guard me with the power of Your grace here and in all places. Now and at all times, forever. Amen.
—St. Augustine, Prayer of St. Augustine

God's love is better than life: better than the best day we've ever had! May we know the overwhelming joy of God's love as we devote our hearts to him in prayer. May we invite the wisdom of his leadership and rejoice at every glimmer of hope we perceive. There is so much beauty to be found in his fellowship!

Today is the perfect day to pursue the Lord with all that we are. Let's give him our attention, our affection, and our adoration. He is the God who brings new life out of the ashes of our disappointment by his restoration power. We have only just begun to know his goodness.

Give praise to the one who loved you more than his own life.

CONTINUAL SATISFACTION

The LORD will guide you continually
and satisfy your desire in scorched places.
ISAIAH 58:11 ESV

We cannot possibly be satisfied with anything less than to walk with God – each day, each hour, and each moment, in Christ, through the power of the Holy Spirit. —Andrew Murray, The Prayer Life

Satisfaction is not the culmination of all things going right in our world. It's not reaching the peak of wealth or comfort. Satisfaction is found in the present moment always, and that is how we cultivate connection with the Lord. Our souls are satisfied as he meets us in the power of the here and now, and we recognize we have all we need for this moment.

The Lord guides us continually as we look to him. His presence is behind and before, and he is with us every step we take. Instead of looking at what we had in the past or what we hope to have in the future, let's refocus our attention on today. How does God meet and satisfy our needs as we walk with him this very day?

Ask the Holy Spirit to direct your attention back to God's presence with you today.

REDIRECTION

You guide me with your advice,
and later you will receive me in honor.
PSALM 73:23-24 NCV

One way to re-collect the mind easily in the time of prayer, and preserve it more in tranquility, is not to let it wander too far in other times: you should keep it strictly in the presence of God; and being accustomed to think of Him often, you will find it easy to keep your mind calm in the time of prayer, or at least to recall it from its wanderings. —Brother Lawrence, The Practice of the Presence of God

When we think of God often, we pray often. As we direct our thoughts to God throughout our day, our souls are enriched and our prayer lives too. We are more easily able to come back to him and offer him the surrender of our hearts.

Our minds wander: we shouldn't feel guilty when they do. The more we learn to remove the judgment from that and simply redirect our thoughts back to the Lord, the more readily we can practice directing our minds and prayers to God. He is always with us.

Redirect your thoughts toward the Lord throughout your day.

TIMELY HELP

God is our refuge and strength,
a helper who is always found
in times of trouble.
Psalm 46:1 CSB

His help is timely. God is our refuge and strength, a very present help in trouble. His help is very wise. He knows how to give each person help that is proper and suitable for him. —C. H. Spurgeon, Faith's Checkbook

God knows exactly what we need every day. When we call on him, we don't call on some generic force that offers the same blanket prescription to all. He is informed, he is wise, and he is helpful in exactly the ways we need him to be.

To resist God's help is to suffer. When we keep ourselves from dwelling in the refuge of his gracious love, we needlessly cause ourselves more worry, pain, and confusion. Instead of struggling to figure things out our way, let's go to the one who knows what we need before we ask.

Instead of struggling today, take each problem you encounter to the Lord, no matter how trivial it may seem to you.

FOUND IN GOD

Not having a righteousness of my own derived from the Law, but that which is through faith in Christ, the righteousness which comes from God on the basis of faith.

PHILIPPIANS 3:9 NASB

If our circumstances find us in God, we shall find God in all our circumstances. —D. L. Moody, Thoughts for the Quiet Hour

The more we dwell in God, the more we find God dwells in and around us. He is everywhere. He is so very near to us, but he is also found wherever we venture. There isn't a circumstance that is left alone by his love. Delight yourself in the Lord, making your heart a welcoming place for him to rest, and you will more easily rest in his delight over you!

May you be found in God today. May the eyes and ears of your heart be open to recognize his fingerprints of mercy. He is already at work in the circumstances you don't know how to fix. Put your faith in him, and trust him. He will not fail.

Pray for greater awareness of God's presence in your circumstances.

ALL IN CHRIST

To me, to live is Christ, and to die is gain.
PHILIPPIANS 1:21 NLT

The more I realize that Christ must be everything to me and that all in Christ is for me, the more I learn to live the real life of faith—dying to self, and living wholly in Christ.
—Andrew Murray, With Christ in the School of Prayer

Faith in Christ is not just seeds of belief. It's action that backs up our beliefs. Everything Jesus did was for our benefit. He paved the way to the Father and broke every chain that held us back. The veil that once separated God's presence from his people has been torn, and we have access to God's liberating love!

Whether we're here living our best in the gracious presence of God, or we've passed on to the eternal realm of God's kingdom, all in Christ is for us. When we truly grasp the power of God's love revealed in Christ, we won't worry about death. As we die to self—to the cycles of shame, fear, and sin—we come alive in the light of Christ.

Pray and ask God for a greater revelation of his heart so you may live wholly in Christ.

ALL THINGS

Of Him and through Him and to Him are all things, to whom be glory forever. Amen.

Romans 11:36 nkjv

Keep reminding God in our times of private prayer that we mean every act for His glory; then supplement those times by a thousand thought-prayers as we go about the job of living.
—A. W. Tozer, The Pursuit of God

Why should we remind God that we mean all that we do, say, and receive for his glory? It is as much a reminder for our own hearts as it is a prayer. We need the perspective shift. When we feel as though our prayers are not about his glory but our own, we can feel the dissonance.

God uses all things for his glory, for he created all things. Prayer isn't a one-time thing and then you're set. When you learn to follow-up with thought prayers as you live, God shines through the cracks of your understanding. The more you reach out to him, the more connected you are and open to hearing his voice.

Humble yourself in prayer and ask for God to be glorified in you as he refines you in the fires of his love.

STARTING POINT

Repent, then, and turn to God, so that your sins may be wiped out, that times of refreshing may come from the Lord.
Acts 3:19 NIV

All the true revivals have been born in prayer.
—E. M. Bounds, Power Through Prayer

No revival has ever happened without prayer, and repentance is a form of prayer. We don't have to wait another day to humble ourselves before God and change our minds and hearts. When we see that there is a way of offense in our hearts or lives, repentance resets us in God's mercy. He is able to redirect the willing heart, but he will not make us change our ways.

Are you at a loss for what to do today? Begin with prayer. Humble your heart in the Lord, and ask him to reveal if there is any habit, belief, or expectation that goes against the ways of his kingdom. Refreshing follows repentance. Personal and corporate revival follow repentant prayer and earnest seeking after the Lord.

Turn to God and offer him all of you. Pray that he'll have his way and follow in repentant obedience.

WHOLEHEARTED PRAISE

I will praise the LORD as long as I live;
I will sing praises to my God while I have my being.
PSALM 146:2 ESV

A Christian should be an Alleluia from head to foot.
—St. Augustine, Expositions on the Book of Psalms

Alleluia is an exclamation of praise to the Lord, and it is an expression of rejoicing. For our whole beings to become an alleluia is to offer God thanks and praise in every circumstance.

It is a powerful practice to give gratitude to God for life, breath, and needs met when we are facing a tremendous challenge. Let's consider this kind of thanksgiving a sacrifice of praise. The more we profess his goodness in our own hearts before we utter a word to others about him, the more we receive his love in the hard places. His love reaches us in the depths of darkness, sickness, and war. He is with us through it all.

Live as a walking, talking alleluia today.

KEEP A LOOK OUT

Do not look out only for yourselves. Look out for the good of others also.

1 CORINTHIANS 10:24 NCV

Never can you be short of themes for prayer; even if no one should suggest them to you, look at your congregation. There are always sick folk among them, and many more who are soul-sick. Some are unsaved, others are seeking and cannot find. Many are desponding, and not a few believers are backsliding or mourning. There are widows' tears and orphans' sighs to be put into our bottle and poured out before the Lord. —C. H. Spurgeon, Morning and Evening

There is no shortage of fuel for prayer when we look around us. Let us remember Christ's example, and follow the wisdom of the Word. We are not only to look out for ourselves, but for the good of others also.

As you go through your day, keep your eyes open for what others are going through. Keep prayer flowing from your heart as you look with eyes of love to partner with God's heart.

Pray for as many people as you can today, really listening and looking for what they are going through.

EXPRESSIONS OF LOVE

The fruit of the Spirit is love, joy, peace, patience, kindness, goodness, faithfulness, gentleness, and self-control.
GALATIANS 5:22-23 CSB

Joy is love exalted; peace is love in repose; long-suffering is love enduring; gentleness is love in society; goodness is love in action; faith is love on the battlefield; meekness is love in school; and temperance is love in training. —D. L. Moody, Secret Power

The fruits of the Spirit each represent an element of love. Why? Because God's very nature is love. When we choose to walk in his ways, love has to become a priority.

Partner with God's presence already at work in you, and take steps of gentleness, peace, joy, faith, meekness, temperance, goodness, and long-suffering. Love cannot be limited, and there is grace for you to grow in the power of God's mercy as you lean on the Spirit and his abundant life.

Pray for the fruit of the Spirit to be evident in your life.

LIVING POWER

What is the boundless greatness of His power toward us who believe.
EPHESIANS 1:19 NASB

We see thus that everything depends on our own relation to the Name: the power it has on my life is the power it will have in my prayers.
—Andrew Murray, With Christ in the School of Prayer

The more submitted we are to Christ, the more powerful our prayers become. The more we know the Lord, the more we realize what's on his heart. He is faithful to save, powerful in help, and ready to meet us as we turn to him with an open heart.

There is boundless greatness in his power. He is able to do all things, and to do them well. Everything flows more easily from a firm foundation of relationship. If we do nothing else today, let's lean into the fellowship of Christ through the Spirit and follow his lead.

What power does Christ have in your life?

GROWING PASSION

"Have I been with you all this time, Philip, and yet you still don't know who I am? Anyone who has seen me has seen the Father!"

JOHN 14:9 NLT

In order to know GOD, we must often think of Him; and when we come to love Him, we shall then also think of Him often, for our heart will be with our treasure.

—Brother Lawrence, The Practice of the Presence of God

Getting to know God isn't the same as knowing about him. We come to the Father through Jesus, and he reveals what God is like. If we struggle to know God, let's come back to the beginning and look at the person of Jesus. Reading through the gospels regularly fills our minds with who he is.

Want to know what to expect from God? Read his Word. Want to walk in the freedom of his love? Follow his example. The more we know God, the more we love him, and the more we love him, the more we think of him. He becomes our greatest treasure, and we pursue him with our hearts and lives.

Pray for increased love as you draw near to God.

SPIRITUAL SECRET

In all things we commend ourselves as ministers of God: as sorrowful, yet always rejoicing; as poor, yet making many rich; as having nothing, and yet possessing all things.

2 CORINTHIANS 6:4,10 NKJV

He had everything, but he possessed nothing. There is the spiritual secret. —A.W. Tozer, The Pursuit of God

The greatest secrets of God are not bought. They are not earned by physical strength. They are found in relationship with him, and he offers that freely. Don't be tricked into thinking anyone else has a short-cut to God's grace. He is the way, the truth, the life, and Jesus is our great mediator. Go to him; nothing stands in your way!

Though we suffer pain in this life, there is still reason to rejoice. No matter the resources we have, we are wealthy when we are rich in the values of God's kingdom. We might have nothing to impress others, and yet we have all we need and more in the grace of God's Spirit.

Pray for the simplicity of his truth to shine in your understanding today.

FLEETING THOUGHTS

Whoever says, "I know him," but does not do what he commands is a liar, and the truth is not in that person. But if anyone obeys his word, love for God is truly made complete in them. This is how we know we are in him: Whoever claims to live in him must live as Jesus did.

1 JOHN 2:4-6 NIV

In the way of GOD thoughts count for little, love is everything.
—Brother Lawrence, The Practice of the Presence of God

Our intentions count for little when we don't put action behind them. We may say we love people, but if we are not known for kindness, generosity, or grace, what does our love really mean?

Jesus said himself that many would come to him saying they knew him, but he would turn them away because they didn't truly reflect his love. Even doing things in Jesus' name does not mean that you have the love of Christ in you. Pray for lives that are full of loving action. When we walk in the ways of Christ, doing as he said and did, we reveal that his love is alive in us.

Pray for specific areas you can show the love of Christ in and put aside empty platitudes.

HIGHEST CALLING

In Christ, there is no difference between Jew and Greek, slave and free person, male and female. You are all the same in Christ Jesus.
GALATIANS 3:28 NCV

This is our high calling, to represent Christ, and act in His behalf, and in His character and spirit, under all circumstances and toward all men.
—A.B. Simpson, Days of Heaven Upon Earth

The highest calling we have in life is to live like Christ lived. Let's lay down every excuse as to why we haven't done it and ask for the grace to follow him. The call to love everyone, including those who hate us, is one that requires humility and grace. Let's put away our pride and offense, and follow the path of love that Christ already laid.

There are no dividing lines in the kingdom of Christ. We are brothers and sisters. We must not be like the world, making differences issues where there aren't any in God's kingdom. We are all loved the same amount in Christ. Let love break down the barriers we have set between us.

Is there a barrier in you that needs to be demolished by love?

PERFECT UNITY

Just as the Lord has forgiven you, so you are also to forgive. Above all, put on love, which is the perfect bond of unity.
COLOSSIANS 3:13-14 CSB

Paul felt deeply for the unity of the body of Christ. He was convinced that unity could only be reached by the exercise of love and prayer.
—Andrew Murray, The Ministry of Intercession

Unity does not happen by accident. It won't be won by arguments or strong stances. It is only through love and prayer that we will have the grace to be one in Christ. When we put the importance of our opinions over the command to love one another, we need to humble ourselves in the presence of God.

The choice to let love cover offenses is a powerful one. In order to be unified, we have to be willing to let love be the highest goal. If the need to be right supersedes this, we let pride build walls between us instead of building bridges of peace. God has forgiven us of more than we could ever repay. Why, then, wouldn't we also forgive others?

Pray for love to be more important to you than the need to be right.

LET IT FLOW

"Give, and it will be given to you. They will pour into your lap a good measure—pressed down, shaken together, and running over. For by your standard of measure it will be measured to you in return."

LUKE 6:38 NASB

Why is it that many Christians are cold? Because they are all the time receiving, never giving out anything. —D. L. Moody, Moody's Stories

God is generous with all he is and has. He withholds no good thing from those who walk in his ways. The same principle applies for us as we live out his example in our own way. The more we are given, the more we have to give to others. There's room enough to receive more as we willingly reflect the generosity of God by giving a portion of what we have to others.

The principle of generosity is not one we should ignore. There is incredible blessing as we pour out God's love through practical acts of generosity. God promises to meet us with more as we share with others. Let's become conduits of his blessings, and let it flow through us!

Ask for opportunities to live generously.

GREAT REWARD

After these things the word of the Lord came to Abram in a vision, saying, "Do not be afraid, Abram. I am your shield, your exceedingly great reward."

GENESIS 15:1 NKJV

Our difficulty seems to be this: the promise is so "exceeding great" that we cannot conceive God really to mean what he clearly appears to have revealed. The blessing seems too vast for our comprehension; we "stagger at the promises, through unbelief," and thus fail to secure the treasure which was purchased for us by Christ Jesus.
—George Müller, The Life of Trust

We cannot fully comprehend the greatness of the reward promised to us through Christ. The great reward we receive is not a mere provision of grace, needs met, or a hope that feels flimsy. Jesus Christ is our great reward, and in him is fullness of love, power, peace, joy, and treasures untold!

Instead of lowering our expectations in God to keep ourselves from disappointment, let's increase them in the reality of God's greatest gift—Jesus Christ.

Thank God for the gift of Jesus Christ, our Great Reward.

LIBERATING TRUTH

"Then you will know the truth, and the truth will set you free."
JOHN 8:32 NIV

He who most clearly discerns the perfect character of Jesus, will be most urgent in prayer for grace to grow like Him.
—C. H. Spurgeon, Prayer and Spiritual Warfare

The more we know Christ, the more we realize his power is what we need in our own lives. His grace is sufficient, his love is liberating, and his truth stands the test of time. He is endless in wisdom and the example of his service is inspiring. We don't have to settle with admiring who Christ was and is. We can experience the power of his life-giving love by living it out.

Jesus' character is lovely. It is not weak, though he was humble. In his unflinching pursuit of the Father and revealing his miraculous love to us, we have the great gift of knowing him more. Let's pray for the grace to grow into the likeness of Jesus as we submit to him each day. Jesus is the truth that sets us free!

Pray for grace to grow in Christ's love.

GLORIOUS TRANSFORMATION

According to the riches of his glory he may grant you to be strengthened with power through his Spirit in your inner being, so that Christ may dwell in your hearts through faith.

EPHESIANS 3:16-17 ESV

The most important discovery of my whole life is that one can take a little rough cabin and transform it into a palace just by flooding it with God. —Brother Lawrence, The Practice of the Presence of God

The humblest places can become the most holy to us when God fills them with his presence. For Brother Lawrence, this was a rustic little cabin. In that place, he met the power of God, and it became to him like a palace, full of glory.

God's presence does this today too. Anywhere we are submitted to his love and asking for his presence to change us becomes transformed by his glory! When the light of God's mercy rises on us like the noonday sun, we are overwhelmed by the beauty of his presence. It transforms the ordinary into glorious chapels of praise!

Ask for an encounter with God's love that leaves you breathless today.

BE FILLED

Instead, be filled with the Holy Spirit.
EPHESIANS 5:18 NLT

It is, therefore, not so much a perpetual fullness as a perpetual filling.
—A. B. Simpson, A Larger Christian Life

Every day we need to fill our stomachs with food to keep us going through the day. Nourishment is something that needs to be tended to whenever our hunger or thirst arises. It is the same with our spirits. We need spiritual nourishment, not because God's presence isn't enough, but because we need to fill up where our energy has been depleted.

If you find yourself needing God's grace, take it as a spiritual hunger cue. If you lack love, go to the source of living water to drink up. Be filled with the Holy Spirit perpetually. God's presence fills you up, then you give out of that fullness, and you go back for more. It is a give and take.

Use prayer as the way to feed your spirit today, going back as often as you need for little snacks along the way.

CHOSEN

This God is the One who gives life, breath, and everything else to people. He does not need any help from them; he has everything he needs.

ACTS 17:25 NCV

Teach us, O God, that nothing is necessary to Thee. Were anything necessary to Thee that thing would be the measure of Thine imperfection: and how could we worship one who is imperfect? If nothing is necessary to Thee, then no one is necessary, and if no one, then not we. Thou dost seek us though Thou does not need us. We seek Thee because we need Thee, for in Thee we live and move and have our being. Amen. —A.W. Tozer, The Knowledge of the Holy

God does not need us to do anything in order to be faithful to his Word. He doesn't need us at all; that wasn't the point of creation. He made us because he wanted to. He loves us, and he chooses to partner with us.

God is perfect in all his ways. God's power is not at all dependent upon you. Take that weight off your shoulders; it's never been yours to bear! You are not needed by God, but he chose you.

If your relationship with God is not about what you offer, what does that mean for your identity in him?

MAKE WAY

Pray also for us that God may open a door to us for the word, to speak the mystery of Christ, for which I am in chains.
COLOSSIANS 4:3 CSB

Prayer opens an outlet for the promises, removes the hindrances in the way of their execution, puts them into working order, and secures their gracious ends. —E. M. Bound, The Possibilities of Prayer

If we want doors to open for the promises of God to come through, we will not wait around casually for them to appear. Where there is passion in our hearts to see breakthrough, let's pray for those open doors to come. Then, we can wait with anticipation knowing that God will lead you at the right time.

Prayer removes hindrances. Sometimes that will look like a door we wanted to open remaining shut. Beautifully, he opens the right door we didn't even realize was there at just the right time, and we will rejoice that we didn't get what we thought we wanted at the time.

When you pray for an open door, is it a specific outcome you envision, or do you trust God to lead you to the right door?

HOPEFUL TRUST

"Behold, God is my salvation,
I will trust and not be afraid"
Isaiah 12:2 NASB

Trust the past to God's mercy, the present to God's love, and the future to God's providence. —St. Augustine, Confessions

As this year comes to a close, consider how you can let it rest in God's mercy. Let go of what you no longer have to carry, and trust God to do what he knows to do. His love is your strength and your song. Don't overlook the beauty that lies within the details of your day.

Now, as you look to the future, trust God's providence and his faithfulness. He knows what is coming, and he will not let you go. He leads you with the confident care of his mercy. You never have to fear what is to come, for he will be with you wherever you go. Trust him to continue to guide you in his goodness.

Thank God for this past year. Pray for grace today, and a bright hope for tomorrow.

QUOTES TAKEN FROM THE FOLLOWING WORKS

Anonymous. *The Kneeling Christian*. London: Pickering & Inglis, 1915.

Augustinus, Aurelius. *Confessions*. Translated by Henry Chadwick. Oxford: Oxford University Press, 1991. Originally *Confessiones*. ca. 397–400 CE.

Augustinus, Aurelius. *Expositions on the Book of Psalms*, translated by A. Cleveland Coxe. Nicene and Post-Nicene Fathers, First Series, Vol. 8. Peabody, MA: Hendrickson Publishers, 1994. Originally *Enarrationes in Psalmos,* written between 392 and 418 CE.

Augustinus, Aurelius. *On the Gift of Perseverance*. Translated by Robert Ernest Wallis. In *The Anti-Pelagian Writings*, edited by Philip Schaff. Nicene and Post-Nicene Fathers, First Series, Vol. 5. Peabody, MA: Hendrickson Publishers, 1994. Originally *De Dono Perseverantiae*, written in 428 CE.

Augustinus, Aurelius. *Soliloquies*. Translated by Rose Elizabeth Cleveland. Boston: Little, Brown, and Company, 1910.

Augustinus, Aurelius. *The City of God*. Translated by Henry Bettenson. London: Penguin Books, 2003. Originally *De Civitate Dei,* written between 413 and 426 CE.

Augustinus, Aurelius. *The Eighty-Three Different Questions*. Translated by David L. Mosher. Washington, D.C.: The Catholic University of America Press, 1982. Originally *De diversis quaestionibus octoginta tribus,* written between 419–426 CE.

Augustinus, Aurelius, attributed by Thomas Shepherd in *The Three Greatest Prayers* (London, 17th c.).

Augustinus, Aurelius. *Tractates on the Gospel of John*. Translated by John Gibb. In *Nicene and Post-Nicene Fathers*, First Series, Vol. 7, edited by Philip Schaff. Peabody, MA: Hendrickson Publishers, 1994. Originally *Tractatus in Evangelium Ioannis*, written between 406 and 420 CE.

Bainton, Roland H. *Here I Stand: A Life of Martin Luther*. Nashville: Abingdon Press, 1950.

Bonhoeffer, Dietrich. *Letters and Papers from Prison*. Edited by Eberhard Bethge. New York: Macmillan, 1953.

Bounds, Edward McKendree. *Power Through Prayer*. Chicago: The Bible Institute Colportage Association, 1910.

Bounds, Edward McKendree. *The Possibilities of Prayer*. New York: Revell, 1920.

Bounds, Edward McKendree. *Purpose in Prayer*. New York: Revell, 1920.

Bounds, Edward McKendree. *The Essentials of Prayer*. Chicago: The Bible Institute Colportage Association, 1915.

Bounds, Edward McKendree. *The Necessity of Prayer*. Chicago: The Bible Institute Colportage Association, 1919.

Bounds, Edward McKendree. *The Reality of Prayer*. Chicago: The Bible Institute Colportage Association, 1920.

Bounds, Edward McKendree. *The Weapon of Prayer*. Chicago: The Bible Institute Colportage Association, 1916.

Brother Lawrence. *The Practice of the Presence of God*. London: J. M. Dent & Sons, 1906.

Bunyan, John. *A Discourse Touching Prayer*. London: Printed for George Larkin, 1663.

Bunyan, John. *Grace Abounding to the Chief of Sinners*. London: George Larkin, 1666.

Bunyan, John. *Mr. John Bunyan's Dying Sayings*. London: Printed for Nath. Crouch, 1688.

Bunyan, John. *The Pilgrim's Progress from This World to That Which Is to Come*. London: Nath. Ponder, 1678.

Calvin, John. *Commentary on the Epistle to the Hebrews*. Translated by John Owen. Edinburgh: Calvin Translation Society, 1853.

Calvin, John. *Institutes of the Christian Religion*. Translated by Henry Beveridge. Edinburgh: Calvin Translation Society, 1845.

Edwards, Jonathan. *An Humble Attempt*. Boston: Samuel Kneeland, 1747.

Edwards, Jonathan. *Hypocrites Deficient in the Duty of Prayer*. Boston: S. Kneeland and T. Green, 1738.

Edwards, Jonathan. *The Life and Diary of David Brainerd*. Edited by Jonathan Edwards. Boston: Samuel Kneeland and Timothy Green, 1749.

Fénelon, François. *Selections from Fénelon*. Translated by Mary W. Springer. Boston: Little, Brown, and Company, 1902.

Françoise-Thérèse Martin, Marie. *The Story of a Soul: The Autobiography of St. Thérèse of Lisieux*. Translated by Thomas Taylor. London: Burns, Oates & Washbourne, 1912.

Gordon, Samuel Dickey. *Quiet Talks on Prayer*. New York: Fleming H. Revell Company, 1904.

Julian of Norwich. *Revelations of Divine Love*. ca. 1395. Edited from the British Library Manuscripts by Marion Glasscoe. Exeter: University of Exeter Press, 1976.

Luther, Martin. *The Large Catechism*. Wittenberg: Joseph Klug, 1529.

Luther, Martin. *Tischreden* [*Table Talk*]. Collected by Johannes Mathesius, Veit Dietrich, and others. First published in Eisleben: Hans Luft, 1566.

Moody, Dwight Lyman. *Men of the Bible*. Chicago: Moody Press, 1900.

Moody, Dwight Lyman. *Moody's Stories: Anecdotes, Incidents, and Illustrations*. Chicago: Fleming H. Revell Company, 1900.

Moody, Dwight Lyman. *Prevailing Prayer: What Hinders It?* Chicago: Fleming H. Revell Company, 1884.

Moody, Dwight Lyman. *Secret Power: The Secret of Success in Christian Life and Work*. Chicago: Fleming H. Revell Company, 1881.

Moody, Dwight Lyman. *Sovereign Grace: Its Source, Its Nature, and Its Effects*. Chicago: Moody Press, 1891.

Moody, Dwight Lyman. *Thoughts for the Quiet Hour*. Chicago: Fleming H. Revell Company, 1900.

Murray, Andrew. *Absolute Surrender*. London: James Nisbet & Co., 1897.

Murray, Andrew. *Experiencing the Holy Spirit*. New York: Fleming H. Revell Company, 1913.

Murray, Andrew. *Humility: The Beauty of Holiness*. London: James Nisbet & Co., 1895.

Murray, Andrew. *Power in Prayer*. Often excerpted from *The Ministry of Intercession*. London: James Nisbet & Co., 1898.

Murray, Andrew. *Teach Us to Pray*. London: James Nisbet & Co., 1895.

Murray, Andrew. *The Inner Life*. London: James Nisbet & Co., 1897.

Murray, Andrew. *The Ministry of Intercession: A Plea for More Prayer*. London: James Nisbet & Co., 1898.

Murray, Andrew. *The Prayer Life*. London: James Nisbet & Co., 1912

Murray, Andrew. *Waiting on God*. London: James Nisbet & Co., 1896.

Murray, Andrew. *With Christ in the School of Prayer*. London: James Nisbet & Co., 1885.

Müller, George. *An Hour with George Müller*. London: S. W. Partridge & Co., 1890.

Müller, George. *Narratives*. London: J. Nisbet & Co., 1845–1898.

Müller, George. *The Life of Trust: Being a Narrative of the Lord's Dealings with George Müller*. Boston: Gould and Lincoln, 1861.

Oatman, Johnson, Jr. "Higher Ground." In *Songs of Love and Praise No. 5*, edited by John R. Sweney, William J. Kirkpatrick, and Henry L. Gilmour. Philadelphia: John J. Hood, 1898.

Sánchez de Cepeda y Ahumada, Teresa. *The Life of Teresa of Jesus: The Autobiography of St. Teresa of Ávila*. Translated by E. Allison Peers. New York: Image Books, 1960.

Simpson, Albert Benjamin. *A Larger Christian Life*. New York: Christian Alliance Publishing Company, 1890.

Simpson, Albert Benjamin. *Days of Heaven Upon Earth: A Year Book of Scripture Texts and Living Truths*. New York: Christian Alliance Publishing Company, 1897.

Simpson, Albert Benjamin. *Standing on Faith*. Harrisburg, PA: Christian Publications, 1910.

Simpson, Albert Benjamin. *The Life of Prayer*. Harrisburg, PA: Christian Publications, 1915.

Simpson, Albert Benjamin. *The Self Life and the Christ Life*. New York: Christian Alliance Publishing Company, 1897.

Simpson, Albert Benjamin. *When God Steps In*. Harrisburg, PA: Christian Publications, 1919.

Spurgeon, Charles Haddon. *According to Promise*. London: Passmore & Alabaster, 1867.

Spurgeon, Charles Haddon. *Characteristics of Faith*. London: Passmore & Alabaster, 1872.

Spurgeon, Charles Haddon. *Comfort for Those Whose Prayers Are Feeble*. London: Passmore & Alabaster, 1875.

Spurgeon, Charles Haddon. *Evening by Evening: A Devotional Classic for Daily Encouragement*. London: Passmore & Alabaster, 1869.

Spurgeon, Charles Haddon. *Faith's Checkbook*. London: Passmore & Alabaster, 1888.

Spurgeon, Charles Haddon. *Hindrances to Prayer*. London: Passmore & Alabaster, 1885.

Spurgeon, Charles Haddon. *Morning and Evening*. London: Passmore & Alabaster, 1865.

Spurgeon, Charles Haddon. *Order and Argument in Prayer*. London: Passmore & Alabaster, 1883.

Spurgeon, Charles Haddon. *Prayer Certified of Success*. London: Passmore & Alabaster, 1882.

Spurgeon, Charles Haddon. *Prayer and Spiritual Warfare: A Collection of Sermons on Prayer*. London: Passmore & Alabaster, 1865.

Spurgeon, Charles Haddon. *Prayer, the Proof of Godliness*. London: Passmore & Alabaster, 1873.

Spurgeon, Charles Haddon. *The Golden Key of Prayer*. London: Passmore & Alabaster, 1884.

Spurgeon, Charles Haddon. *The Great Revival: Addresses Delivered at the Monday Evening Meetings in 1859*. London: Passmore & Alabaster, 1859.

Spurgeon, Charles Haddon. *The Saint and His Saviour*. London: James Nisbet & Co., 1857.

Spurgeon, Charles Haddon. *The Soul Winner*. London: Passmore & Alabaster, 1895.

Spurgeon, Charles Haddon. *The Throne of Grace*. London: Passmore & Alabaster, 1887.

Spurgeon, Charles Haddon. *The Treasury of David*. 7 vols. London: Passmore & Alabaster, 1869–1885.

Taylor, Dr. and Mrs. Howard. *Hudson Taylor's Spiritual Secret*. London: China Inland Mission, 1932.

Thomas à Kempis. *The Imitation of Christ*. Translated by William Benham. London: J. M. Dent & Sons, 1907.

Torrey, Reuben Archer. *The Baptism with the Holy Spirit*. Chicago: Moody Press, 1895.

Torrey, Reuben Archer. *The Person and Work of the Holy Spirit*. New York: Fleming H. Revell Company, 1910.

Torrey, Reuben Archer. *The Power of Prayer and the Prayer of Power*. Grand Rapids: Zondervan, 1924.

Torrey, Reuben Archer. *How to Pray*. Chicago: Moody Publishers, 1900

Tozer, Aiden Wilson. *Of God and Men*. Harrisburg, PA: Christian Publications, 1960.

Tozer, Aiden Wilson. *Paths to Power*. Harrisburg, PA: Christian Publications, 1949.

Tozer, Aiden Wilson. *The Attributes of God: A Journey into the Father's Heart*. Chicago: Moody Press, 1961.

Tozer, Aiden Wilson. *The Knowledge of the Holy*. New York: Harper & Brothers, 1961.

Tozer, Aiden Wilson. *The Pursuit of God*. Harrisburg, PA: Christian Publications, 1948.

Tozer, Aiden Wilson. *The Root of Righteousness*. Harrisburg, PA: Christian Publications, 1955.

Tozer, Aiden Wilson. *Worship: The Missing Jewel of the Evangelical Church*. Harrisburg, PA: Christian Publications, 1961.

Watson, Thomas. *A Divine Cordial*. London: Thomas Parkhurst, 1663.

Watson, Thomas. *The Doctrine of Repentance*. London: Thomas Parkhurst, 1688.

Watson, Thomas. *The Godly Man's Picture Drawn with a Scripture Pencil*. London: Thomas Parkhurst, 1666.

Watson, Thomas. *The Lord's Prayer*. London: Thomas Parkhurst, 1692.

Watson, Thomas. *The Ten Commandments*. London: Thomas Parkhurst, 1692.

Wesley, John. *A Plain Account of Christian Perfection*. London: Printed by R. Hawes, 1777.

Wesley, John. *Covenant Prayer*. In *The Works of John Wesley*, Vol. 11: *The Appeals to Men of Reason and Religion*. Edited by Thomas Jackson. London: Wesleyan Methodist Book Room, 1872.

Wesley, John. *Explanatory Notes Upon the New Testament*. London: Printed by William Bowyer, 1755.

Wesley, John. *Letter to Mrs. Bennis*. In *The Letters of the Rev. John Wesley, A.M.*, Vol. 4. Edited by John Telford. London: The Epworth Press, 1931. Originally written in 1768.

Wesley, John. *The Character of a Methodist*. London: Printed by William Strahan, 1742.

Wesley, John. *The Means of Grace*. London: Printed by William Strahan, 1746.

Wesley, John. "Upon Our Lord's Sermon on the Mount (Discourse Ten)." *The Christian Advocate and Journal,* 1755.